W9-BYI-765

ALSO BY MEGHAN DAUM

THE UNSPEAKABLE

THE UNSPEAKABLE

AND OTHER SUBJECTS OF DISCUSSION

8/4 D24U

MEGHAN DAUM

FARRAR, STRAUS AND GIROUX   NEW YORK

Farrar, Straus and Giroux
18 West 18th Street, New York 10011

Library of Congress Cataloging-in-Publication Data
Daum, Meghan, 1970– author.
    [Essays. Selections]
    The unspeakable : and other subjects of discussion / Meghan Daum. —
First edition.
        pages   cm
    ISBN 978-0-374-28044-4 (hardback) — ISBN 978-0-374-71006-4
(e-book)
        I. Title.
PS3604.A93 A6 2014
814'.6—dc23

2014014643

Designed by Jonathan D. Lippincott

Farrar, Straus and Giroux books may be purchased for educational, business,
or promotional use. For information on bulk purchases, please contact the
Macmillan Corporate and Premium Sales Department at 1-800-221-7945,
extension 5442, or write to specialmarkets@macmillan.com.

www.fsgbooks.com
www.twitter.com/fsgbooks • www.facebook.com/fsgbooks

10 9 8 7 6 5 4 3 2

CONTENTS

THE UNSPEAKABLE

INTRODUCTION

For more than twenty years now I have been making something of a specialty of writing about myself. I still have mixed feelings about the whole genre. In some respects, serving as my own main subject has been a great convenience. It saves me money on travel, research fees, and even potential litigation (I cannot sue myself for libel, though once or twice I've imagined confronting myself at a party, asking, "How could you say those things!" and throwing a drink in my face). In other respects, though, it feels lazy. We all have a few good yarns in us, but I tend to think most of the best ones make the narrator a peripheral character rather than the star of the show. The best ones come from the outside world, where careful listening and a resistance to preconceptions can yield stories that do all the things we want and need stories to do—split sides, break hearts, open minds or even change them.

I've written a lot of outside stories, too. For nearly a decade, I've been a newspaper opinion columnist, covering subjects ranging from national politics to sexual politics to the cultural significance of the U.S. Postal Service. I've done magazine reporting on military spouses caring for veterans with traumatic brain injury, and on young people throwing themselves into the bacchanal of spring break in Cancún. I've written profiles of celebrities I'd previously never heard of. Years ago, I wrote website copy for a line of feminine hygiene products, a job whose requirements included making cold telephone calls to accomplished businesswomen asking if they would be willing to be featured as the site's "Woman of the Month." I could offer them no monetary compensation, though one candidate asked if she might be paid in the form of feminine hygiene products—alas, she could not.

But for all my ambivalence about mining my own life for material, I can't seem to quit for very long. In the end, the work I always come back to, the work that seems best remembered and draws the strongest reactions, is the work in which the "outside world" forms a vital partnership with that *I* narrator. And this book is nothing if not a testament to that partnership. All of these essays have been written in the last few years, not on assignment for any periodical but for the sole purpose of appearing in this book, in the company of one another. They were not published elsewhere before this book came into being, not even in a "slightly different form," the phrasing often used to describe material that has been repurposed from short to long form or vice versa. Prepublication sneak previews aside, you're seeing them here first.

For much of the time I worked on this project, when people would ask me what it was about I would say that it was a book about sentimentality. I would say that the essays covered a range of subjects—death, dogs, romance, children, lack of children, Joni Mitchell, cream-of-mushroom-soup casserole, to name a few—but that collectively I hoped they'd add up to a larger discussion about the way human experiences too often come with preassigned emotional responses. I wanted to look at why we so often feel guilty or even ashamed when we don't feel the way we're "supposed to feel" about the big (and sometimes even small) events of our lives. I wanted to examine the ways in which so many aspects of contemporary American life—where we live, who we love, when or if we choose to settle down with a partner, what we eat, why we appreciate the art and music and literature that we do, how we expect to die and what we expect of the dying—seem to come shrink-wrapped in a layer of bathos.

For all the lip service we pay to "getting real," we remain a culture whose discourse is largely rooted in platitudes. We are told—and in turn tell others—that illness and suffering isn't a ruthless injustice, but a journey of hope. Finding disappointment in places where we're supposed to find joy isn't a sign of having different priorities as much as having an insufficiently healthy outlook. We love redemption stories and silver linings. We believe in overcoming adversity, in putting the past behind us, in everyday miracles. We like the idea that everything happens for a reason. When confronted with the suggestion that life is random or that suffering is not always transcendent we're apt to not only accuse the suggester of rudeness but also pity him for his negative worldview. To reject sentimentality, or even question it, isn't just uncivilized, it's practically un-American.

As I wrote more of the book, however, I began to realize that sentimentality and its discontents were only part of the picture. The primary subject, if there can be said to be one, is simpler than that. At its core, this book is about the ways that some of life's most burning issues are considered inappropriate for public or even private discussion. It's about the unspeakable thoughts many of us harbor—that we might not love our parents enough, that "life's pleasures" sometimes feel more like chores—but can only talk about in coded terms, if at all. It's about the unspeakable acts that teach no easy lessons and therefore are often elbowed out of sight. In some places, the book is about literally not being able to speak. It's about what happens when words fail in the truest sense.

This book also recounts some pretty unflattering behavior on my part, not to mention a few disclosures about my interior life that some readers will probably find depressing or even alarming. That is fine. I wouldn't have it any other way. In fact, I suspect this is the kind of book that winds up being loved and hated in equal measure. I'd be thrilled if that was the outcome, actually. When I teach writing students, I often tell them that nobody will love their work if some people don't also hate it. They always look stunned, even terrified, as if I've just told them they'll never meet their soul mate unless they also make a mortal enemy of someone. Then more often than not they have a "breakthrough" and start handing in stories about certain bodily functions involving the lower digestive tract. Fortunately, most writing workshops are pass/fail.

Back in 2001, also known as light-years ago, I published an essay collection called *My Misspent Youth*. In the foreword I reminded readers that the essays were not confessions, that the material I was plumbing was "about me but also a lot of other things." The same is true of this book, and while I don't need to point out that the essays can be filed under all sorts of categories apart from "author looking in the mirror" (and, for the record, there are no stories heavily featuring either the upper or lower digestive tracts), I do feel compelled to say again that, as frank as they are, they aren't confessions. Not even close. They're events recounted in the service of ideas. My aim was to judiciously choose and arrange episodes that might build upon one another and add up to something interesting enough to warrant the time it takes to read about them. And while some of the details I include may be shocking enough to suggest that I'm spilling my guts, I can assure you that for every one of those details there are hundreds I've chosen to leave out.

Speaking of leaving things out, just so we're clear, I've changed the names of most of the people I write about in these pages. This is primarily for the sake of their privacy, though I think most of them are good-enough sports that they wouldn't mind (or in some cases might even have preferred) if I'd disclosed their identities. The handful of celebrities who show up in these essays appear under their real names, as it seems a bit pointless to try to disguise Nicole Kidman as someone named "Jane." This is not, obviously, a book of straight reportage. I am recounting events to the best of my memory. I have not tried to reproduce conversations and quotes verbatim, though I made a point of resisting the temptation to reimagine situations and lines of dialogue as anything simpler or snappier than they actually were. To have done so would not only have made my work more complicated than it needed to be but also betrayed the central duty of most of these essays, which is to examine the tension between primal reactions and public decorum. This book is about the spin we put on our lives. So I'm giving it to you as straight as I can.

MATRICIDE

People who weren't there like to say that my mother died at home surrounded by loving family. This is technically true, though it was just my brother and me and he was looking at Facebook and I was reading a profile of Hillary Clinton in the December 2009 issue of *Vogue*. A hospice nurse had been over a few hours earlier and said my mother was "very imminent." She was breathing in that slow, irregular way that signals that the end is near. Strangely, I hadn't noticed it despite listening for the past several weeks (months earlier, when her death sentence had been officially handed down but she was still very much alive, my mother had casually mentioned that she'd noticed this breathing pattern in herself and that I should be prepared to walk into the room and find her gone at any moment) but apparently it was here now and when I reached the third paragraph of the second page of the Hillary Clinton article (this remains imprinted on my brain; I can still see the wrap of the words as my eye scanned the column; I can still see the Annie Leibovitz photo on the previous page) I heard her gasp. Then nothing more.

"Mom?" I called out.

My brother got off the couch and called her name, too. Then I said, "Is that it?"

That was it. I found suddenly that I wasn't quite sure how to identify a dead person—it didn't occur to me in that moment that not breathing was a sure sign—so I picked up her hand. It was turning from red to purple to blue. I'd read about this in the death books—*Final Gifts, Nearing Death Awareness, The Needs of the Dying*—that I'd devoured over the last few months. Medically speaking, I'd found these books to be extremely accurate about how things progressed, but some put a lot of emphasis on birds landing on windowsills at the moment of death or people opening their eyes at the last minute and making amends or saying something profound. We weren't that kind of family, though, and I harbored no such expectations. I had been slightly worried that when my mother actually died I'd be more grief-stricken than I'd anticipated, that I'd faint or lose my breath or at least finally unleash the tears that I'd been unable to shed all this time. I thought that in my impatience to get through the agonizing end stages I'd surely get my comeuppance in the form of sneaky, shocking anguish. Perhaps I would rage at the gods, regret all that had gone unsaid, pull an article of clothing from her closet and hold it close, taking her in. But none of that happened. I was as relieved as I'd planned to be. I picked her hand up a few more times over the next two hours while we waited for another hospice worker to come over and fill out the final paperwork and then for the men from the funeral home to take her away. I did this less for the sake of holding it than to make sure she still had no pulse. She'd chosen cremation but had said once that she feared being burned alive.

A woman worked for us during the last two months of

my mother's illness. She must have found us appalling. A week or so before my mother died, my brother and I started packing up the apartment right in front of her. I know this sounds grotesque, but we were hemorrhaging money and had to do whatever we could to stem the flow. It was late December and her lease was up on the first of the new year. If she died before then and we didn't have the place cleared out, we'd not only have to renew the lease and pay another month of sizable rent, but we'd also have to then go on to break the lease and lose her sizable security deposit. She was unconscious, so "right in front of" is a matter of interpretation, but her hospital bed was in the living room and we had to crouch behind it to remove books from shelves. My mother had a set of George Kovacs table lamps that I liked very much, and every time I look at them in my own house now, three time zones away in a living room she's never seen, I think about how I had to reach around her withering body to unplug them, after which I packed them into their original boxes, which I'd found deep in her coat closet, walked them over to the UPS Store, and mailed them off to California.

"You have to start sometime," said Vera, the woman who worked for us. I'm almost certain she said this because she had no idea what to say but felt some obligation to validate our behavior since we were paying her $17 per hour. Vera was a professional end-of-life home health care aide, referred to us by hospice. She was originally from Trinidad and spent a lot of time listening to Christmas music on headphones. I assumed she'd known every kind of family and witnessed every iteration of grief, though later I learned she'd worked for only one other terminal patient in New York, a man who was dying of something other than cancer and whose daughter apparently cried all the time and threw herself on his empty hospital bed after he was taken away. Our family, as my mother might have said, had "a significantly different style."

My mother died the day after Christmas. She was sixty-seven years old. She lived on the Upper West Side of Manhattan, where she'd moved three years earlier after retiring from her job as a high school theater teacher and director in New Jersey. She had an exquisitely decorated one-bedroom apartment that she couldn't really afford, though, true to her nature, she had a number of business and creative projects in the works that she trusted would change her financial equation. These included theater coaching for Broadway hopefuls as well as potentially mounting a play she'd written (her first literary endeavor) that she told me she felt could hit the big time if only she got it into the right hands. But in January 2009, after months of complaining of pain in her side and being told by her doctor it was probably a pulled muscle, she was found to have gallbladder cancer. This sounds like the kind of thing you could easily cure by just removing the gallbladder, which everyone knows is a nonessential organ, but it turns out the disease is not only extremely rare but barely treatable. Not that they weren't going to try.

The week of my mother's diagnosis, her own mother died at age ninety-one. This wasn't as calamitous as you might think. "I don't really feel anything," my mother said when she told me the news. "I lost her so long ago." Technically she was referring to the dementia my grandmother had suffered for several years but we both knew that the real loss existed from the very beginning. My grandmother was tyrannical in her childishness. She was stubborn, self-centered, and often seemingly willfully illogical. Though she didn't overtly mistreat my mother, I'm fairly certain that my mother saw her as a neglecter. Not in the sense of failing to provide food and shelter but in the sense that is knowable only to the neglectee, and even then maybe never entirely. I'm tempted to say that my grandmother damaged my mother on an almost cellular level. But then again maybe some of my mother's damage was her own. She freely admitted that from the age of fourteen until she left her parents' house after college, she stopped speaking almost entirely when she was at home. In the outside world, she won piano competitions and twirled the baton, but inside the house she offered nothing more than an occasional mumble. I think the idea was that her mother was so unwilling to listen to her that she was no longer going to waste her breath.

As a very young child I'd taken the requisite delight in my grandparents; they had candy dishes and cuckoo clocks, plus they lived far away and I saw them only once a year at the most. But as I grew older and my grandfather died and my mother lost what little buffer had once stood between her and her adversary, the more I came to see the pathology that swarmed around my grandmother like bees. She was a mean little girl in a sweet old woman's body; she spoke about people behind their backs in ghastly ways, sometimes loudly just seconds after they'd left the room. She spoke in a permanent whine, sometimes practically in baby talk. My mother, whose life's mission was to be regarded as serious and sophisticated, recoiled from this as though it were a physical assault. She often said she believed her mother had an "intellectual disability." For my mother's entire life, her mother was less a mother than splintered bits of shrapnel she carried around in her body, sharp, rusty debris that threatened to puncture an organ if she turned a certain way.

We didn't need to have my grandmother's funeral right away, my mother said. It would require travel to Southern Illinois, a ragged, rural place out of which my grandmother had seldom set foot and from which my mother, despite having left at twenty-three, never felt she could totally escape. Like me, my brother lived in Los Angeles, though unlike me, it was hard for him to get away from work and no one expected him to just drop everything to attend his grandmother's funeral. My father, though sort of in the picture in that he also lived in Manhattan and was still married to my mother, was not in any picture that would have required him to make this trip. My parents had been separated for nearly twenty years, beginning around the time my mother began to self-identify as a theater person and potential single person, though they'd never bothered to divorce. The rest of us, though, would go the following month, when my brother could request a few days off and after my mother was recovered from her surgery and had gotten in a round or two of chemotherapy. It would turn out to be the last trip she ever took. At the memorial service, she addressed the small crowd of mostly eighty- and ninety-somethings about how far she'd moved beyond Southern Illinois but how she still appreciated it as a good place to have grown up. This was entirely untrue, since as far back as I can remember she'd blamed a large portion of her troubles on her hometown as well as on her mother. Also untrue was the notion, which my mother had let grow in her hometown some years earlier and never bothered to tamp down, that she was single-handedly responsible for the career of a famous actor who had gone to the high school where she'd taught. In truth, the actor had dropped out before she began working there, but my brother and I nodded and went along with it.

In our family, being good children did not have to do with table manners or doing well in school but with going along with my mother's various ideas about herself and the rest of us. Mostly they amounted to white lies, little exaggerations that only made us look petty if we called her out on them so we usually didn't. Or at least we didn't anymore. There was a period of at least fifteen years, from approximately age eighteen to age thirty-four, when every interaction I had with my mother entailed some attempt on my part to cut through what I perceived as a set of intolerable affectations. The way I saw it, she had a way of talking about things as though she wasn't really interested in them but rather imitating the kind of person who was. What I always felt was that she simply didn't know how to *be*. She reminded me a bit of the kind of college student who's constantly trying on new personalities, who's a radical feminist one day and a party girl the next, who goes vegan for a month and doesn't let anyone forget it, who comes back from a semester in Europe with a foreign accent. Not that she actually was or did any of these things. It was more that she always felt to me like an outline of a person, a pen-and-ink drawing with nothing colored in. Sometimes I got the feeling she sort of knew this about herself but was powerless to do anything about it. She wanted to be a connoisseur of things, an expert. She wanted to believe she was an intellectual. Once, among a group of semistrangers, I heard her refer to herself as an academic. Later, when I asked her about it, she told me she appreciated college towns and academic-type people and therefore was

one herself. When I asked her what she thought an intellectual was, she said it was someone who "valued education"
and preferred reading to sports.

What was my problem? Why couldn't I just let it go, laugh
it off, chalk it up to quirkiness rather than grant it status as a
legitimate source of my barely contained rage? For starters,
her need for praise was insatiable. And around the time of
her emancipation from her old self, when she moved out of
the house and seemingly took up permanent residence in the
high school theater, that need redoubled. We never gave her
any credit, she said. We always put her down, didn't take her
seriously. And now that she "felt really good" about herself
(for dressing better, for going blond, for losing weight, for
having a career), we couldn't bring ourselves to be happy for
her. That she was completely right about all of this only added
to my rage. We couldn't give her any credit, at least not enough.
She just wanted it too badly. She'd ask for it outright. In heated
moments, she'd practically order me to praise her as though I
were a child being told to clean my room. "It would be nice if
just once you'd just say, 'Hey, Mom, you're really good at what
you do,'" she'd tell me. "If you'd say, 'You do that *so very* well.'"

If you asked me what my central grievance with my
mother was, I would tell you that I had a hard time not seeing
her as a fraud. I would tell you that her transformation, at
around age forty-five, from a slightly frumpy, slightly depressed, slightly angry but mostly unassuming wife, mother,
and occasional private piano teacher into a flashy, imperious,
hyperbolic theater person had ignited in her a phoniness that
I was allergic to on every level. I might try to explain how the
theater in question was the one at my very high school, a place
she'd essentially followed me to from the day I matriculated
and then proceeded to use as the training ground and later

backdrop for her new self. I might throw in the fact that she was deeply concerned with what kind of person I was in high school because it would surely be a direct reflection of the kind of person she was.

Thanks to my own need to please others and draw praise, my life in high school became a performance in response to my mother's performance. When I saw her approaching in the hall I'd grab a friend by the elbow and throw my head back in laughter so she'd perceive me as being popular and bubbly. When I did poorly on a test I followed her advice and didn't let on to anyone. Meanwhile she copied my clothes, my hair, my taste in jewelry, so much so that I started borrowing her things (they were exaggerated versions of my things: skirts that were a little too short, blazers with massive shoulder pads, dangling, Art Deco–inspired earrings) because it seemed easier than trying to pull together my own stuff. In the years to come, my mother would become the go-to teacher for the sexually confused and the suddenly pregnant. But in the nascent stages of her coolness, I wasn't allowed out past ten o'clock. She found it embarrassing that I had a boyfriend. This was beneath me, an unserious pursuit, especially since he wasn't involved in the arts. She didn't want to be known as someone whose daughter would have a boyfriend in high school. She liked when I waited for her at the end of the day so she could drive me home, even (perhaps especially) if it meant my having to pace around the theater while she finished up her business.

Kids whose parents are teachers in their schools are members of a special club. They have to build invisible fences. They have to learn to appear to take it in earnest when their classmates tell them how cool the parent is. They have to learn not to take it personally when they aren't privy to the pot smoking in the boiler room. I never considered myself a member of that club. In those years, my mother seemed to have just slipped through the door as I walked through it on the first day of school. It was never entirely clear what she was doing. She had no theater experience; her background was in music. It made sense that she was volunteering as a piano accompanist, playing in the pit orchestra, coaching singers. It made less sense that she always seemed to be there even after the musicians went home. Hanging out with the set builders, feigning disapproval when kids banged out pop songs instead of the assigned show tunes on the piano, giving more and more orders until everyone just assumed she was in charge.

In all the years that came before, when I was three and six and ten and fourteen, my mother had cautioned me not to be dramatic, not to overaccessorize, not to be "the kind of kid who's always *on*." "That doesn't show a lot of substance," she'd say. *Substance* was one of her all-time most used words; in both of her incarnations she used it liberally, though her powers of appraisal were questionable. A man we knew who was brilliantly insightful, well-read and well-spoken—a true intellectual—came across to her as lacking in substance because he told hilarious stories about what a screwup he'd been in college. She believed Barbara Walters showed substance on *The View* when she hushed the other ladies up and spoke her mind.

In the last twenty years of my mother's life, I think I can count on one hand the times when she did not have a delicate, artisan-woven scarf tossed around her neck. In her entire lifetime I don't think I ever once heard her laugh out loud.

There was no more clothes sharing after I left for college. During that time my mother moved out of our house and into her own place and I came home as infrequently as possible, staying with my father when I did. Her career in full throttle, she was usually too busy for family time anyway. She was out late rehearsing summer stock productions of *Sweeney Todd*. She had close friends whose names I didn't know and would never learn. Still, my assignment from there on out was clear. For the rest of her life, what I was supposed to do was celebrate how little my mother resembled her own mother. I was supposed to accept that her old personality had been nothing more than a manifestation of various sources of oppression (her mother, her husband, the legacy of 1950s Southern Illinois) and that what we had on our hands now (the fan club of gay men, the dramatic hand gestures, the unsettling way she seemed to have taken on the preening, clucking qualities of a teenage girl, almost as if to make up for skipping over that phase the first time) was the real deal.

I could not, however, manage to do those things. Even more cruelly, I couldn't even fake it. She had a habit of picking up the phone in her office inside the high school theater and letting the receiver hang in the air for several seconds as she continued whatever in-person conversation she was already having. When she did this to me I usually just hung up. On the occasions when I visited the theater, I smiled silently when her students gushed about her superfabulousness. Several times I told her flat out that if I, as a kid (who had been instructed at the age of six to answer the phone, "Hello, this is Meghan Daum," and then "professionally" field the call to the appropriate parent), had for even one second exhibited the traits of her new personality, her former personality would have sent me to my room for three months.

"I wish you'd been raised by the new me," she said more than once.

The last time I saw my grandmother was almost ten years before she died. I visited her with my mother. Arriving at her apartment, which was in a sterile two-story complex near the main highway of the town she'd never left, my mother and I were immediately taken into her bedroom and shown her latest collection of teddy bears. They were dressed in clothing that said things like "God Bless America" and "I Hate Fridays." My grandmother's speech had the thick, Ozarks-influenced twang endemic to Southern Illinois—a "hillbilly" accent, my mother always called it—and as she cooed over the bears and pronounced this one "real purdy" and another one "cute as can be," I saw my mother's hands curling into tight, livid little fists. They were the same fists I made whenever I heard the outgoing message on my mother's answering machine, which for the nearly twenty years she lived alone had somehow rubbed me as the most overarticulated and high-handed version of "leave a message after the tone" in the history of human speech.

(My mother told me that when she was a girl she secretly unwrapped her Christmas presents ahead of time and then rewrapped them and placed them back under the tree. The reason for this was that she didn't trust herself to react appropriately to them. She had to plan in advance what she was going to say.)

My grandmother's infractions went deeper than stuffed animals, of course; and while I might be able to cite my mother's central grievance—that her mother didn't recognize her accomplishments, didn't appreciate the person she was, didn't, in fact, see her at all—I'd be a fool to think I had any real grasp of the terrain of their relationship. During that last visit, while my mother was describing in detail the complexities of her latest theater production, my grandmother interrupted her mid-sentence and asked, "Honey, do you ever wish you'd been a career gal?"

You'd think something like that maps out the terrain pretty well—"Jesus Christ, what do you think she's been talking about?" I snapped as my mother fumed silently—but no one can ever truly read that map, maybe especially not even those occupying its territories. A lot of people knew my grandmother to be as nice as pie, just as a lot of people knew my mother as an incredibly talented theater arts administrator and overall fun person to be around. Neither of those observations was objectively wrong, they just weren't the whole story. But there again, what can you say to that? In the history of the world, a whole story has never been told. At my grandmother's burial site, my mother broke away from the crowd and stood alone at the headstone looking mournful and pensive. I recognized my cue and walked over and put my arm around her, knowing this would create a picture she wanted people to see and would therefore console her. Not that anyone could see the real source of our grief, which was not my grandmother's absence but the limited time my mother now had to enjoy that absence. My mother would die nine months later, and what most people don't know is that of all the sad things about this fact, the saddest by far is that she did not have one day on this earth in which she was both healthy and free of her mother. All her life she'd waited to be relieved of the burden of being unseen, only to have that relief perfectly timed with her own death sentence.

·

My father understood this cruel twist, though at times he
seemed to understand little else. He did not, at least to my
knowledge, bother to look up *gallbladder cancer* on the Internet when it first entered our family lexicon and see that the
average life expectancy after diagnosis is five months and
that fewer than 2 percent of patients make it to the five-year
mark. Since he lived a twenty-minute cab ride away and
since their relationship, for all its animus, still extended to
things like hospital visits and accompaniment to chemotherapy appointments, he did do his share of emptying buck-
ets when she vomited and showing up at the emergency
room when she had a crisis of pain or hydration. Our family
was not one to shirk its duties, even if we did not always
perform them warmly.

Curiously, though, my father did not seem particularly
affected when, after eight months of aggressive chemotherapy at a major cancer center that prided itself on beating the
odds, the news was delivered that the treatment was no longer
working—"longer" referring to the three months beyond
the average my mother had survived. She would likely die
within half a year's time (it turned out to be two months).
There were many ways my mother could have chosen to tell
my father she was dying and there were many ways he could
have chosen to respond. Their choices, as my mother lay in
her hospital bed and I sat nearby in my usual visitor's chair,
playing around on my laptop computer as usual, were these:

"The timeline has been moved up," my mother said.

"I see," said my father.

"So they're talking months at this point."

"Hmm. Okay."

"So what else is going on?" my mother finally asked when
it was clear he wasn't going to say anything more.

"Well, actually, I have done something to my foot," my father said. "I somehow stumbled when I got out of bed and stepped down on it the wrong way. And it's been killing me."

My mother said maybe he should have it looked at.

"He's happy," she hissed after my father left the hospital on his aching foot. I told her that wasn't true, that he was scared. I said this not because I believed it but because it seemed like the kind of thing you should say.

I could try to go into the reasons why my parents never got divorced but I suspect that would fall into the category of trying to explain fully how things were between my mother and my grandmother or even my mother and myself, and that would be overreaching, moot, a fool's errand. I could try to explain all the ways that my father is a good person who behaved the way he did partly because he lacked the "emotional vocabulary" to face the situation and partly because my mother, who'd hired a van and moved out of the house on a humid summer day in the early '90s, could never make up her mind about what she wanted from him. For years, she'd summoned him when she needed him—to mark holidays, to suggest to out-of-town guests that their marriage was not exactly over but simply had "a different style"— and shunned him pretty much the rest of the time. When she got sick, a few ferociously loyal friends from her old personality came in from New Jersey whenever they could, though no one would have held it against them if they hadn't. But the gay man posse, not to mention the friends my mother had claimed to have made since moving into the city ("a costume designer who has many inroads to theater producers," "a *very* interesting museum curator," "so many former students who live here now but still want my advice"), were largely absent and so it was that she was forced to call on my father for help and he obliged, though not as graciously as she would have liked. When I hopped on a red-eye flight at a moment's notice because it was clear she needed to go to the famous cancer center's urgent care unit but didn't want my father to take her, my presence was tacitly understood as a polarizing force. My mother felt grateful and vindicated. My father felt snubbed.

"You didn't have to come out here, you know," he told me as we loitered around the vending machines. "I've taken her before. I'm capable of it."

He wasn't capable of it. He didn't know the code. Or, if he did, he refused to abide by it. I can't blame him. The code had to do with not just showing up but actually being there, which was no longer really a part of their social contract. My mother didn't want my father to be her husband but she still wanted him to impersonate one when the occasion arose. All around us were family members of other patients, people who sobbed in the hallways or set up camp at bedsides or emerged from the elevators carrying piles of blankets and needlepoint pillows and framed photos from home. One afternoon, en route to the visitors' kitchenette to get coffee, I passed a man clutching the door handle of a utility closet and crying. He looked to be in his sixties. He looked weathered and hammered down, as if he'd spent his life doing manual labor. I assumed he was crying over his wife, though I had no idea. No one was crying like that for my mother. Occasionally I'd overhear family members of other patients using words like *gift* and *blessing*, words they seemed to be able to use without apologizing for sounding sentimental. Our family had a significantly different style. We weren't bringing anything up in the elevator except our own lunch. Occasionally I brought up flowers or a book I knew she'd never read, which is to say I understood the code enough to fake it.

The best line in this whole saga goes to my mother's oncologist, who broke the bad news like this:

"Our hope for this treatment was that it would give you more time. Some of that time has now passed."

One day some months earlier I had entertained a passing fantasy that my mother would get hit by a bus. The oncologist had just delivered the news that the chemotherapy was working. This came as a surprise, since an earlier therapy had failed and this was plan B, which I'd assumed stood even less chance. My mother was elated and shifted at once into one of her more dramatic gears, calling friends and telling them she was on the road to recovery, that it appeared she was a special case, that the doctors "were so pleased." She was so happy that day that she actually ventured outside the apartment on her own to buy a Frappuccino and I remember thinking to myself how great it would be if she were hit by, say, the M7 express on Columbus Avenue and killed instantly and painlessly. I knew from the Internet that chemotherapy for gallbladder cancer works (when it works at all) for about one cycle before the body develops immunity and the disease resumes the process of ravaging it. She would never have a better day than this day. She would never again walk down the street feeling as hopeful and relieved and exceptional as she had when she strode out of the doctor's office that morning, past the throngs of chemo patients and their families sprawled out in the lounge like stranded airline passengers, past the ever-friendly lobby personnel (trained, no doubt, to greet each visitor as if it were the last greeting they'd ever receive), and on to the street, where for the first time in weeks she actually hailed a cab herself and announced her desire for a Frappuccino.

That night she drank half a vodka gimlet to celebrate and regretted it for the next several days. She vomited from the chemo through the rest of the summer until she landed back in the hospital with severe intestinal and bowel trouble. It was September. Autumn, New York's most flattering season, was preparing to make its entrance. I had just gotten engaged to my longtime boyfriend, which had made my mother very happy.

"Our recommendation would be to transfer to another level of care," the oncologist said.

Hearing this, I moved my chair closer and grabbed my mother's hand under the blanket. I did this because I felt that if we were in a play this would surely be part of the stage directions. I was also afraid the doctor would judge me if I didn't. If I just sat there with my arms crossed against my chest, as I was inclined to, the doctor would make a note in the file suggesting that I might not be capable of offering sufficient support to the patient.

I retrieved her hand from under the blanket and squeezed it in my own. She did not reciprocate. She didn't pull away, but there was enough awkwardness and ambivalence coming from both sides that it was not unlike being on a date at the movies and trying to hold hands with someone who'd rather not. I think we were both relieved when I let go. The doctor said she would most likely make it through Christmas, so we should feel free to go ahead with any holiday plans.

For three nights in a row, my mother made me stay in her hospital room. She was dealing with incontinence (if you

learn nothing else from these pages, learn that gastrointesti-
nal cancer is not the kind of cancer to get; get any other kind,
even lung, even brain, but don't get carcinoma of the gut)
and it had grown so severe that she was up every few minutes
and sometimes didn't make it to the bathroom in time. The
people who came to clean her up were terse and tired and
spoke mostly in heavy Caribbean accents. A few times she lay
there in her own shit before they could get there. I know this
because I was in the sleeping chair on the other side of the
room, listening to it all while pretending to be asleep.

I tell myself now, as I told myself then, that if things had
gotten really bad, if she had cried out in pain or called my
name or if a serious amount of time had passed before a staff
member came, I'd have gotten up and helped her. I tell myself that I closed my eyes to protect her dignity, that if she
could step back from the situation she'd never want me wip-
ing her shit, that there are some daughters in the world who
would do this for their mothers but that we had never been
that kind of mother and daughter and trying to pretend to
be so now would only make both of us feel inexpressibly and
inerasably violated. I tell myself I did it out of compassion but
the truth is I also did it, as I had done so many other things
where she was concerned, out of rage. I was enraged at her
for her lifetime of neediness that she'd disguised as a million
other things—independence, fabulousness, superiority—and
demanded praise for. I was enraged at how this bottomless
longing encircled her like barbed wire and that now that she
genuinely and rightfully needed me I just couldn't deliver. I
was enraged that what I was doing struck me as so unspeak-
ably cowardly that when I was finally allowed to return to
her apartment and order Chinese food and drink from the

wine stash she hadn't touched in ten months I wouldn't even be able to call my fiancé in Los Angeles and say what I'd done.

Later, when the horror of those nights had been eclipsed by other horrors—patient proxy forms, calls to an attorney, wrenching phone conversations with her friends—my mother was discharged from the hospital and my father and I took her back to her apartment in a taxi. I'd been in taxis countless times with my mother since her ordeal had begun, mostly taking her to or from a chemo session, and it seemed that invariably the driver was playing a talk radio station sponsored heavily by cancer treatment centers. This day was no exception. "I got my life back," a voice earnestly intoned. "So say goodbye to cancer and hello to a front-row seat at your granddaughter's wedding." My mother would have no grandchildren. Neither my brother nor I had ever shown an interest in reproducing. I had a dog, which she sometimes called her granddog. The three of us sat in silence through this advertisement and several others—for weight loss, for acne scar removal, for adjustable mattresses. It was a cold, gusty day and tree branches scraped the car while we waited at red lights.

Back at the apartment, my father stood around awkwardly for a while, and finally left.

"Would you do all this for him?" my mother asked me. "Would you take care of him?"

One thing I did for my mother that I would not have done for my father was get married. That is to say, I got married pretty much right then and there, less than six weeks after getting engaged, so she could be in attendance. We spent three weeks discussing the wedding and five days actually arranging for it, which in retrospect I think is the perfect amount of time to plan a wedding. During the time we were discussing it my mother became fixated on hosting the event in her apartment and inviting her friends and associates. Due to limited space, this would exclude many of my and my fiancé's friends and associates. She also made it clear she did not want children in her apartment for fear of their knocking over her pottery or damaging her art. My fiancé made it clear he didn't want to get married in a dying woman's apartment. He did not make this clear to the dying woman herself but to me during the countless hours I sat with my cell phone in the lobby of the famous cancer center's hospital trying to figure out how to handle the situation of a dying woman (a woman dying brutally and prematurely) who effectively wanted to turn her only daughter's wedding into a funeral she could orchestrate and attend herself. Meanwhile my mother, who'd heretofore thought my fiancé walked not only on water but on some magical blend of Evian, San Pellegrino, and electrolyte-enhanced Smartwater, began to say things like "Well, now I'm seeing a different side of him." When I pointed out to her that he'd like the wedding to include his sister's small children, she told me he had to realize he couldn't always get what he wanted.

The discussion period ended when my mother realized she was too sick to orchestrate anything. She told me to wait and get married after she was gone—"It happens all the time," she said, crying. This was one of our more authentic conversations because it so happened that I authentically wanted her there. My father, as far as I could tell, regarded marriage as a fatuous institution. In moments, he seemed to regard my wedding plans as yet another complication that had been thrown into the mix of our crisis. My mother was the only person on earth for whom my getting married really meant something. She was the only one for whom it wasn't a take-it-or-leave-it kind of thing. I felt like it wouldn't count if she weren't there. It was the first thing I'd needed her for in a long time and the last thing I'd need her for from there on out. So on a Sunday in late October we rounded up everyone we could and walked from my mother's apartment to the park across the street, where we were married by a close friend who'd been ordained online the day before. Photos taken by another close friend later suggested my mother was in an extraordinary amount of pain. Wearing a wig, being humiliatingly pushed along in a wheelchair by my brother (with whom, a month later, at Thanksgiving, I would trade earsplitting obscenities as she lay in the next room after vomiting at the dinner table), she is wincing in every shot. In some, she's not only wincing but also staring into space. After seeming relatively alert during the preshow (champagne at her apartment, compliments on the decor), she appeared to unravel throughout the ceremony, shifting from barely living to officially dying in the time it took me to slip from lack of official attachment into wedlock. The next day, the four members of the hospice team came to the apartment to introduce themselves. When they asked her to describe her level of pain on a scale from one to ten—one being no pain, ten being unbearable—she told them eight. When we asked if she was really sure about that she said she wasn't sure. She said she had never in her life been able to answer that sort of question.

A few times I saw Vera kneeling by my mother praying. I ducked away and pretended not to see but I appreciated the gesture nonetheless. Bedside praying wasn't something I'd ever done myself, though when my mother was still cogent I'd told her a secret I've told maybe two other humans ever. I'd told her that I'd prayed most nights since I was nine years old (prompted by extreme guilt over a schoolyard incident in which I'd caused another child to burst into tears) and found it a useful tool for, if not speaking to a higher power per se, articulating that for which I was most grateful and that for which I most hoped ("Thank you for letting me pass the French test; please get me through math class tomorrow"). I added that I usually tried to send out a special prayer to someone who probably needed it (the girl I'd inadvertently made cry, the stray animals of the world), at least if I didn't fall asleep first.

Given our belief system (atheist) and overall family dynamic (cynical, avoidant of confrontation yet judgmental behind people's backs), this was an extremely vulnerable thing to share. It didn't entirely pay off. "That sounds like a nice ritual," my mother said before going back to staring at the television (in an echo of her own mother that would have horrified her, she never changed the channel and watched anything that came on: the news, the weather, *The Price Is Right*). Other times, when she seemed particularly aware of the irreversibility of her situation, I'd turn off the TV and try to get philosophical. I told her that as presumptuous as it might be to believe in an afterlife it was equally presumptuous to deny the possibility of one. Then, at the risk of mockery or at least disapproval, I said that I felt like reincarnation was at least something worth thinking about, that it felt clear to me that souls existed and that you could just tell from knowing people that some souls had been around longer than others. Plus, dogs obviously had souls, so there you had it.

"Maybe you'll have a whole new life and it'll be even better than this one," I said.

"But I don't want to be a baby again," she said. Her voice sounded genuinely worried.

Ironically, she was in adult diapers. Women's Depends, size small. I'd been sent to the drugstore to buy them on numerous occasions, especially when she was in the hospital and didn't like the brand they had there. I suspected she'd been using them for several months now, actually. Back in the summer, when she was still thinking she might be cured, I'd walked into her apartment and thought odors from the young children who lived upstairs were somehow migrating downward. Months later I realized those children were all too old for diapers.

"Maybe you won't have to be a baby again," I told her. "Maybe you'll be a bird. You'll fly around and look at everything from up high."

"I don't want to be a bird," she said.

It's amazing what the living expect of the dying. We expect wisdom, insight, bursts of clarity that are then reported back to the undying in the urgent staccato of a telegram: *I have the answer. Stop. They're waiting for me. Stop. Everyone who died before. Stop. And they look great. Stop.* We expect them to reminisce over photos, to accept apologies and to make them, to be sad, to be angry, to be grateful. We expect them to clear our consciences, to confirm our fantasies. We expect them to get excited about the idea of being a bird.

My mother's official date of death was December 26 but the day she actually left was December 5. This was the day her confusion morphed into unremitting delirium, the day the present tense fell away and her world became a collage of memory and imagination, a Surrealist canvas through which reality seeped in only briefly at the corners. Suddenly she seemed no longer in pain. She was mobile, even spry, and given to popping out of bed as if she'd forgotten to take care of some piece of essential business. When I walked into her bedroom that morning, a painting had been removed from the wall and clothes she hadn't worn in months were strewn across the floor. She'd thrown up, of course, and the green-brown vomit was dribbling down her pajamas and onto the bed. Whereas the day before she'd have been flustered and embarrassed, she now seemed unfazed, unapologetic, even ecstatic. She wanted her purse, she told me. She needed to put some things in it. I recognized this impulse from my death books. Dying people often pack suitcases and retrieve their coats from the closet because they're overcome with the idea that they're going somewhere. My mother had a cane she used for the rare occasions when she got up—a tasteful wooden thing; she'd refused the walker sent over from the medical supply company—and now she had it in bed with her and was waving it around so it threatened to knock over the lamp and yet more pictures. When I leaned over the bed to wipe up the vomit, she put the end of the cane on my head and began rubbing my hair. She was smiling a crazy smile, her tongue hanging from her mouth like an animal's. The gesture struck me as something an ape might do if you were sitting across from it trying to make it play nicely with blocks, a helpless molestation, a reaching out from behind the bars of a cage. When I managed to grab the cane she resisted for a moment before letting it go.

"Meghan," she said solemnly. Her voice over the last few weeks had grown faint, her speech slurred and monotone. It was the sound of fog rolling in over a life.

"What, Mom?" I chirped. She could hear just fine but I'd taken to talking loudly, as if she were an old person who was going deaf. It drove her crazy. She was always shushing me.

"We need to figure something out here."

"What's that?"

"I need to ask you something."

"What?"

"How did we get kidnapped?"

The dying have their own version of dementia. They drift not only between the real and the not real, the past and the present, but also the living and the dead—and not just the dead they appear to be seeing but the dead the living want to believe they're seeing. It's like they're living in six dimensions, at least two of which exist solely for the benefit of the people standing around watching and listening to them. ("Folks with dementia say the darnedest things!") "Is that Grandpa you're talking to?" we ask when they murmur at an empty chair. "Is there someone up there? Tell me!" we plead when they lift their arms in the air and curl their hands over invisible shapes. Science says the grasping gestures are related to changes in brain chemicals as the body shuts down, but my death books said it's because dying people reach up to greet those who died before them. A cat visited my mother regularly in her final weeks, at one point jumping on her bed and lying at the foot of it like every cat we had when I was growing up. In the beginning, I'd laughed and told her there was no cat, but with the dying you soon learn the folly of raining on a parade, especially one that might produce that holy grail of darnedest things: insight into the afterlife.

"What kind of cat is it?" I asked, finally. "Is it orange?"

"Black," she rasped.

We'd had two orange cats, both named Magnificat and called Niffy for short. Niffy One and Niffy Two, both of which were friendly and affectionate. In between we'd also had a black tomcat that was an asshole.

My mother softened in senility. She developed a childlike quality she probably hadn't had even as an actual child. Her head seemed perennially cocked to one side, her eyes wide, and with her hair now growing back in soft white tufts she looked like a perfect white frosted truffle. For the first time in years, she was without affectation. There was no trace of the drama queen. As feathery and ephemeral as she was, she seemed like a real person rather than someone impersonating her idea of a person. Though I never would have said it, she looked almost exactly like her mother, who, despite her fleshiness and thick glasses and suspected intellectual disability, everyone, even my mother herself, had recognized as being very pretty. For the first time in years, I didn't merely love her. I actually liked her.

"Do you know why you're here?" the hospice nurse asked her gently one day (unlike me, she knew not to shout). This was turning out to be a day of particularly acute agitation. There was a lot of picking at the sheets and furious murmuring. I'd long given up my philosophical lectures. My new best friend was Haldol, which was supposed to keep her calm and which I administered under her tongue through a syringe. There was a perverse and momentary pleasure in this act; it made me feel like I was a stern, efficient nurse, like someone who knew what she was doing.

Her words, barely intelligible, were like soft formations carved from her teeth and lips. Her breath could scarcely carry them an inch.

"Because," she said, "my mother was here."

Ten months after my mother died, twenty months after my grandmother died, I nearly died myself. Oddly enough, this was a scenario that had crossed my mind a time or two over the preceding year. Talk about a morbid trifecta: three generations of women in one family, each of them almost physically repelled by the one before, wiped out in less than two years' time. This wasn't a recurring thought, more like the kind of thing that crosses your mind two or three times and then convinces you that the sheer act of thinking about it at all converts it from a mere implausibility to an almost total impossibility. This is what doomsday scenarios are for. They protect us from disaster by playing out the disaster ahead of time. They're the reason the plane doesn't crash and the bomb doesn't drop. They're the reason we will almost certainly not die in childbirth. The fact that I almost died despite having entertained the thought of dying, the fact that my organs began to fail despite my having walked down the snowy sidewalks in the days after my mother's death, thinking, *Maybe you're next, maybe there are no coincidences, maybe you were right about it being presumptuous not to believe in an afterlife and maybe the afterlife of this matriarchal line is a group-entry kind of deal*, still feels at once too overwhelming and too silly to fully contemplate. And yet it became relevant to the story of my mother's death and my grandmother's death before that. In fact it's part of the same

story, a third act that got rewritten at the last minute, a nar-
rowly dodged bullet from the gun that went off in the first.

It started with a fever. Actually it started before that. Of
course it did. Nothing ever begins when you think it does.
You think you can trace something back to its roots but roots
by definition never end. There's always something that came
before: soil and water and seeds that were born of trees that
were born of yet more seeds. The fever may have been the
first thing I bothered to pay attention to but there was so
much before that. It's possible I'd been getting sick all along,
that my immunity had begun slowly eroding from the week
my grandmother died and my mother became a cancer patient. Throughout it all, I hadn't so much as gotten a cold.
But in October 2010, right around the one-year mark of the
wedding and the screaming at Thanksgiving and the buying
of Depends and the administering of the morphine and then
the Haldol and then the methadone, I returned to New York
for a visit. I wanted to attend a friend's wedding, see the leaves,
escape the taunting, pitiless heat of autumn in Southern
California. It was my first time back in New York since my
mother had died and I thought it might be possible to claim
the streets as my own again, to seal the preceding eighteen
months in plastic and toss them in a trash can where they
could await collection alongside the Greek paper coffee cups
and the dog shit.

The fever was perplexing, as I am rarely sick, so rarely in
fact that I didn't have a primary care doctor at home in Los
Angeles, much less in New York, where I'd lived during my
entire twenties without health insurance. Not that there
seemed any need for one. It was the flu, obviously. The only
cure was time and fluids. For three days I staved off the fever
with aspirin, huddling under blankets in a friend's Brooklyn

apartment and canceling one plan after another. But time was curing nothing. Each day I woke up to more weakness and more fever, body aches that felt like I'd been thrown down the stairs the day before, thirst that no amount of orange juice could quench.

The day after returning to Los Angeles I went to a walk-in clinic, where I was put on an IV for rehydration, told I had a nasty virus, and sent home. The next day I couldn't stand up and my eyes were yellow. I returned to the clinic and was put on another IV and then in an ambulance to the nearest hospital, where I was asked what year it was and couldn't think of the answer. Formless, meaningless words rolled out of my mouth like worms. There was no grabbing on to them. They had no edges, no consonants, no meaning. A doctor came and held his fingers up and asked me to follow them. He furrowed his brow as he wrote notes in his chart. When my husband showed up from work I was suddenly compelled to express grave concern for a friend back in New York. She was the last person I'd seen before I got the fever. We'd had dinner in Carroll Gardens and then I'd stopped at a drugstore for vitamin C pills. Now, after closing my eyes in a hospital bed and then waking from a half-sleep involving some half-dream in which this friend was being held against her will (metaphorically speaking, that is; it was as if I were witnessing her life from afar and seeing all the ways in which she was an indentured servant—to her husband, to the publishing business, to New York City itself), the words fell from my mouth like food dribbling down a baby's chin. Somewhere in my mind there was a concept, an urgent, hulking, planetlike idea that I had to get out. But it seemed composed of invisible gases. It was an abstraction within an abstraction and now it was sliding out of my line of vision the way the landmarks drift past the windows of an airborne plane. Still, I had something to say.

"Listen to me," I slurred. "I need to tell you something. We have to help Sara."

The words came out as *lishen to me* and *we hava help Shara*.

I do not recall being in any pain or even being terribly anxious. Instead, I was mortified. I sounded exactly like my mother. The voice coming from my parched mouth might as well have been a recording of her voice on the day she rubbed her cane in my hair. Even in my delirium, I cringed the way adult children cringe when they look down and realize the hands sticking out of their arms are actually their parents' hands. I remember thinking that everyone was onto me now. My husband, the doctor, whoever else was there: they all knew not only that I was my mother's daughter but also that I was no different from her. Just as she had outlived her own mother by less than a year, I, too, would be denied a life outside of her shadow. The message was so obvious it might as well have been preordained: no woman in this matriarchal line would escape punishment for not loving her mother enough, for not mourning her mother enough, for not missing her enough, for refusing to touch her. None of us would be allowed out in the world on our own.

Apparently this had all happened on a Wednesday. It's the last thing I remember before waking up on what I was told was Sunday. It would be several more days before I understood that they'd put me in a medically induced coma and I'd almost taken things a step further by dying.

People who'd been milling around the hospital, bringing my husband food he couldn't eat and asking questions no one could answer, would later want me to tell them what had happened during the four days I was out. Had there been a white light? Had I encountered any dead relatives? Had I experienced anything that would move me to radically change my life? When I couldn't come up with anything interesting I started to wonder if the random thoughts I'd had in the half-awake state of the postcatatonic, prelucid days that followed my transfer out of the ICU were actually remnants of a near-death narrative. In those days I'd started to think, for instance, that if I survived whatever had happened (and we didn't know what had happened until my ninth day in the hospital) I'd get my act together and behave like an adult. I would, for instance, stop being so bratty about finding the perfect piece of real estate. (My last conversation with my husband, before I grew too sick to converse, had been yet another argument over how much we were willing to overpay to remain living in the inflated, rapidly gentrifying neighborhood where we'd recently sold my tiny, rather ramshackle single-girl house and which I believed to be the only neighborhood in the continental United States where I could be happy.) I'd forgive my father (who'd gotten on a plane for L.A. around the time I'd been put in the coma) for complaining about his foot. I'd make an effort to be closer to my in-laws, who I'd heretofore never thought to call on my own volition. (My father, for his part, had managed to go his entire married life without ever initiating a conversation with my mother's mother or even addressing her by name.)

I even, to my great shock, entertained the thought of having a baby. I'd never really wanted one. For about a million reasons, it had barely scraped the bottom of my to-do list since approximately the seventh grade. My husband knew this, but I'd always suspected that one of the pacts of our marriage was an unspoken belief that I might change my mind. And the more I learned about how sick I'd been—it seemed I'd had swelling of the brain, multiple organ failure, and a severe platelet disorder that required several transfusions; it seemed my wrists were bruised not because of medication, as I'd suspected, but because I'd been placed in restraints after trying to pull out my breathing and feeding tubes; it seemed there'd been a very real possibility that I'd die and an even greater possibility that if I didn't die, I'd have brain trauma that would require long-term rehabilitation; it seemed that throughout all this my husband had left my side only to use the bathroom and to phone anyone he could think of who might know who the best brain trauma specialists were—the more I thought that refusing to have a child was fatuous at best and gratuitously defiant at worst. After all, who says I'd be as negative and judgmental a parent as I'd always assumed I'd be? Who says I'd shudder at the sight of toys in my quiet, uncluttered, grown-up rooms? Who says I'd be as nervous and angry as my own mother had been, that the damage incurred by her own mother would trickle down and sting my eyes just enough to blind me to the damage I myself was inflicting? Who says my old maxim on this subject would turn out to be right, that if I had a child I would certainly love it but not necessarily love my life. Who was saying this but me? No one, of course. And who was I to be trusted?

Miraculously (this was the word they used), I got better fast enough to leave the hospital after eleven days. The diagnosis, in a nutshell, was freak illness. A bacterial infection gone terribly awry. I went home and slept for two weeks. Two months later my husband and I bought a house in a neighborhood other than the one I'd insisted on living in. It had twice as many bedrooms as we had people in our household;

it was owned by the bank and we got it for cheap. Within a month of moving in, a few weeks after my forty-first birthday, I was pregnant.

I was neither excited nor dismayed. I told myself that now that my mother wasn't around to make me feel guilty for not being sufficiently impressed with her, I could find it within myself to be impressed with a child. I told myself there was plenty of room in the house, that I wouldn't have to give up my study if we could combine the den and the guest room, that it was perfectly acceptable to be sixty years old by the time your kid graduated high school. I told myself I'd raise the kid to be strong and independent and to not need me. I'd send it to summer camp and maybe to boarding school. I'd encourage it to make the kind of friends who stick around, to find a community and stay there, maybe even to marry young. I'd ensure that if I died at sixty-seven the kid would be able to pack up those George Kovacs lamps around my decaying body and not feel too bad about it. I thought of it as "it" even though I was sure it was a boy. I was also sure all these provisions were unnecessary because the thing itself wasn't going to stick around.

It didn't. It was gone after eight weeks. I was neither relieved nor devastated. There'd been an element of impostordom to the whole thing, as though I'd spent two months wearing the wrong outfit. The lab results came back the way they usually do for forty-one-year-olds who miscarry: chromosomal abnormalities, totally nonsurvivable, nothing that could have been done. When I asked the doctor if it was possible to know what sex it would have been, she told me that it would have been a girl. I was shocked for a moment but then not. Of course it was a girl. It was a girl and of course it was dead, another casualty of our fragile maternal line, another pair of small hands that would surely have formed furious fists in the presence of her mother. Except this one was gone before she even got here. Maybe she'd joined the others somewhere. Maybe she'd already become a bird. Maybe she'd circle back to me someday and reattempt her landing. Or maybe, better yet, she was the quick, quiet epilogue at the end of our story. Not that I'll ever know what this story is about. I know only that I'll probably never finish telling it and it most certainly will never be whole.

THE BEST POSSIBLE EXPERIENCE

I once dated a man who read astrology books, believed in chakras, and worked regularly with a spirit guide, a communion that involved visiting a "spirit guide counselor" at her modest townhouse near San Diego and paying her to chant and beat drums while he lay on a massage table wearing flashing LED sunglasses. This man was very spiritual. He spoke often of his "teachers," by which he meant not high school or college teachers who had exerted particular influence but various yoga and meditation instructors who I now suspect he'd had sex with. He went to the Burning Man festival every year in a giant RV. He had a "home yoga practice" that chiefly involved lying on the floor of his bedroom and "centering his energy." He was a student of erotic massage. He was into "breath work."

He took me to the spirit guide counselor one time. He said he wanted me to understand him better, and because my anthropological curiosity often trumps my common sense (and because he was covering all costs, including the scenic Amtrak ride down the coast from L.A.), I agreed. The counselor, who, if I recall, charged $200 for a forty-minute session,

asked me a few things about myself: what were my greatest
fears, what was my most cherished memory, what were my
most pressing issues at the moment. Though my most pressing issue was that I was dating someone with whom I had
spectacularly little in common and somehow hadn't yet gotten around to breaking up with, I told her that I had "commitment issues" generally. She handed me the glasses and had
me lie down on the massage table. She told me to tell her what
colors I became aware of as she chanted and beat the drums.
The visual effect was a lot like what happens when you press
down on your eyelids. I told her I saw a lot of black and some
yellow. She took out a steel triangle and struck it with a mal-
let. She took out a cowbell and rang it several times. After
about half an hour she told me to go into the living room and
wait while she received the message from my spirit guide. My
gentleman friend was sitting on the sofa flipping through the
most recent issue of *Variety*, which he'd brought with him.
He explained that the counselor always provided a full-page,
single-spaced report that she typed up on her computer in a
postsession fury of divine dictation.

Soon enough she came in with the results. She said I was
the reincarnation of the spirit master Lord Lanto, an ascended
master who serves as the ruler of the Second Ray of the solar
presence. This is the ray of wisdom, and it vibrates as the color
yellow. On the train ride home, I read my report:

> Blessings and praise to you, Divine Meghan. You are
> indeed a star child. But you are so much more than
> that. You are an ascended master who has chosen to
> incarnate this lifetime to assist the planet in its time
> of transition . . . Life on earth has been a little bit dif-
> ficult for you to adjust to. You come from a much

more advanced civilization and it is hard for you to understand how humans can do the things they do to one another in the name of God and in the name of love. This is why you shy away from committed and close relationships . . . It will be good for you to see the spirit guide counselor again as soon as possible because she is the accelerator and the awakener. You need to have a private session so your needs can be more easily met.

That's just an excerpt, but you get the gist.

My paramour seemed pleased by this, as Lanto was known to emanate an intense golden aura from his heart center, which was visible to those who had "learned through deep practice how to see," and which he had noticed on me recently while we were watching television. For his part, his work with the spirit guide counselor had long ago established that he was the reincarnation of Jesus Christ.

This man was one of those people who don't just think or believe in things but are *about* things. *Let me tell you what I'm about,* he said on one of our earlier dates. He was about "spontaneity" and "acceptance." He was about "being in the moment." One time, in the midst of a discussion over how I should design my new business cards, he suggested I incorporate a pattern of circles, such as he had done on his own self-designed cards. When I said, "I don't like circles, I like squares," his body caved in a bit, and he looked hurt. "If you don't like circles," he said, "you don't like me."

Like most of us, this man was full of contradictions, though whereas in some people contradictions can add to overall interestingness, the effect in his case was mostly exasperating. For all his disciplined mellowness, he erred more than a little on the side of obsessive compulsion. Though it's hard now to believe our relationship advanced to the air-travel stage, we ended up taking a trip to New York, where we stayed at the Hilton Towers in midtown Manhattan. Upon our arrival, he decided he didn't like our room and requested a move to a higher floor. He made this decision after we'd been in the room a solid fifteen minutes, enough time for him to unpack his suitcase and not only hang his shirts and pants in the closet but also fold his socks and underwear and sweaters into neat stacks in the dresser drawers. When I suggested to him that all of the rooms in this thirty-six-story hotel were pretty much identical he told me that we were paying guests and deserved our money's worth (which happened to be $140 per night via Priceline.com). He called the front desk and requested a room change and soon a bellman arrived to escort us to a higher floor.

Upon inspection of the new room, my friend decided he didn't like the desk chair in the new room as much as the one in the old room and asked if they could be swapped out.

"Are you kidding me?" I asked.

"I just want to have the best possible experience," he said.

"Well, you are not asking this gentleman to go switch the chairs," I said, glancing sheepishly at the bellman.

"Then I'll do it myself," he said. He then rolled the chair out into the hallway and accompanied the bellman down the elevator to the first room. Ten minutes later, he returned with the previous desk chair, which had armrests whereas the other did not.

I'm a little hazy on the details of the rest of this trip. However, I do remember sitting in silence at the airport while

Desk Chair, a perfectly able-bodied forty-year-old, insisted on preboarding our return flight along with "those in need of special assistance" because he wanted to secure more overhead space and was not above lying about having a back injury. (I refused to partake in this scheme and we boarded separately.) And though I have tried many times to forget, I'm afraid I also recall quite vividly that, upon our arrival in L.A., I somehow ending up riding in the backseat of my own car as we left the airport.

When I try to piece together exactly how this happened, my best guess is that I'd started off in the passenger seat (apparently we'd achieved the level of intimacy signified by one person feeling comfortable driving the other's car) but reached behind me to find a dropped item and, not locating it, actually crawled into the backseat. By the time I found whatever it was (my cell phone, if I had to bet on it), we had exited the airport and were merging onto the freeway. And though I should have simply climbed back into the passenger seat without announcement I instead asked for permission (in a "will it distract you if I step over the console now?" kind of way), and Desk Chair told me it wasn't safe to move around in a speeding car. When I asked if he meant that I should remain in the backseat for the rest of the forty-minute drive he said something to the effect of "I guess so." And so I rode in my own backseat going east on the 105 freeway and north on the 110 past the L.A. Convention Center and the luminous, blocky skyscrapers of downtown. I rode in my own backseat as we headed northwest toward Hollywood on the 101 freeway and then exited onto the dark, scabrous streets of the then still-a-little-funky, still-gentrifying neighborhood where we both lived because we were single and "creative"

and this was where single, creative people lived if they wanted
to surround themselves with—and potentially date and possibly marry—like-minded folk.

   Desk Chair and I parted ways shortly after that. He found
a woman who liked circles, married her, and had a child. I
took a year off from dating after that, during which time
I cut my hair even shorter than it had been previously and
proceeded to look a great deal like a lesbian even though I
had little interest in actually being one. When I grew tired
of that racket I slowly began growing my hair out, holding
back my shaggy bangs with little bobby pins* and, almost
overnight, attracting men again. In relatively quick succes-
sion, I dated a lawyer, a film producer, a medical resident,
and a couple writers. Then I met my husband. In less than a
week, I knew he was the person I was supposed to marry. I
knew this because of a certain (somewhat tasteless, though
delicious to me) joke he cracked during our very first conversation and the way his apartment was taken up mostly by
surfboards and old copies of *The New York Review of Books*. I
also knew that I wouldn't have wanted to meet him even a
day earlier than I did. I wouldn't have been ready. I was at
that time thirty-six years old.

   You might be thinking that I had a severe case of arrested development. Thirty-six (my husband was a tender
thirty-five) is a fairly geriatric age at which to decide you're
mature enough to settle down (and in fact we didn't feel mature enough to actually get engaged until more than three
years later, at which point we had a bittersweet incentive to

---

*Collectively dubbing these pins, which had tiny, sparkly flowers and butterflies on
the tips, "the barrette that changed my life," I remarked to a friend that the sudden
male attention might be the result of "being better able to see my face." She snorted
and said, "No, it's because men like the little-girl look."

not drag our feet, because my mother was dying). You might also be thinking, based on my rather astonishing lack of agency in the relationship with Desk Chair, that I was relatively inexperienced with men at the time.

But here was the thing about my dating life. I spent most of it with absolutely no eye toward making a permanent commitment. What I was in it for, what I was *about*, was the fieldwork aspect. I wasn't looking to be delivered from the lonely haze of bachelorettehood into the smug embrace of coupledom. I was looking for experiences, for characters, *for people who paid other people to chant and beat drums while they lay on massage tables wearing flashing LED sunglasses.* I regarded my love interests less as potential life mates than as characters in a movie I happened to have wandered into. I suppose that I had some version of a physical type (Roman nose, Eastern European descent, a predilection toward plaid flannel shirts) but for every man who checked these boxes there were others who veered off the page entirely. I dated an airline pilot (conservative Catholic, ex-military, resident of Florida) who said "mind-bothering" when he actually meant "mind-boggling." I lived for nearly three years with a wannabe mountain man who subsisted on what he earned from odd jobs and did not have a bank account. I also, despite the seemingly large number of men I've referred to, spent a whole lot of time not dating anyone at all—more time, I daresay, than most of the other single people I knew. (A cast of characters this plentiful is less a function of being promiscuous than of not meeting your future spouse until you are thirty-six.)

These experiences brought about many headaches and arguments and lectures from friends—"But he's so limited!" "You can't bring him anywhere!" "He believes the earth is three thousand years old!" My friends were often right. Some of these relationships were slightly ridiculous, but I am certain that they made me a more interesting person than I would have been if I'd limited my dating pool to more conventionally suitable men. As for the conventionally suitable men I did spend time with, I've peered at enough of their lives through the rosy portal of Facebook to get a sense of what could have been had I not dispatched them (or, just as often, they dispatched me) over some real or imagined evidence of incompatibility. And though I've admired their beaming children and their comely, accomplished wives and the stainless-steel appliances and apron-front sinks that make quiet, satisfied appearances in the backgrounds of photos snapped spontaneously at the family breakfast table, I've never come away feeling anything other than happiness for their apparent happiness.

The way I'm wired, I was never going to settle down before I did. If I had met my soul mate at twenty-four or even twenty-nine or thirty-three, I would have left him before things got too serious. I had boxes to check that I believed were bigger than any relationship. I wanted to get far enough in New York City to live without roommates. I wanted to leave New York City and move someplace very unlikely. I wanted to wring as many experiences as I could out of the unlikely place and then move to Los Angeles, where I would buy a house by myself and live in it with my dog and no one else. Upon reaching this point, I reasoned, I would be exponentially more fascinating than I'd been at any of the earlier junctures and therefore able to attract a similarly fascinating person. To have stopped at any point along the way would have been to quit the race too soon. It would have caused me to be an inferior person living an inferior life. This is what I tell myself, anyway. This is what I tell my husband when he says he wishes we had met earlier. This is an integral part of my personal mythology and I'm sticking to it.

A few years ago I was asked to take part in a panel discussion on the subject of marriage. The central questions had to do with what might be considered the best time to get married and whether nuptial-delaying heathens like myself represent a trend that may be good for us as individuals but ultimately Bad For America. The panel was being organized by the director of an outfit called the National Marriage Project, a research initiative designed to study marriage and its relationship to society and public policy (and then advocate for it strongly). The Project was trying to promote a new report called "Knot Yet: The Benefits and Costs of Delayed Marriage in America" and, as the director put it, to "start a dialogue." The participants in this dialogue would be two of the report's authors, one of whom directed the National Marriage Project itself, and two woman writers from L.A., one of whom was me. Each speaker would present ten to fifteen minutes of remarks before the panel discussion began. As the report's authors were both family men with religious leanings and other red state sensibilities (not that they announced themselves as such), my job was to comment on their findings and represent the "female point of view" or the "urban point of view" or, at the very least, "another perspective." For this I would be paid a generous and un-turn-down-able sum of $2,500.

The perspective on which I was supposed to provide some kind of alternative was the theory posited by the Marriage

Project that "delayed marriage" (they cited the statistic that the average age of first marriage is twenty-seven for women and after twenty-nine for men) was beneficial to the educated middle and upper middle classes, especially women in these classes, but had deleterious effects on the non-college-educated population. The reason was that less-educated people (defined as those with only high school and some college and referred to in the report as "Middle Americans") were skipping the marriage step but going ahead and having children anyway. The report identified two models of marriage. There was the "capstone" model, which sees marriage as a kind of reward for accomplishing any number of personal and professional goals, or, as they put it, "having your ducks in a row." And then there was the "cornerstone" model, which sees marriage as the foundation and starting point from which you build a life.

The capstone model is fine, the research suggested, if you're talking about people who are going to follow through and actually get married when they finish law school or get that Ph.D. The problem is that only a third of the nation's population has a four-year college degree. The other two thirds might aspire to a capstone marriage, but never quite get around to it because they can't rise out of their low-wage jobs. They often go ahead and have children, though.

The National Marriage Project thought this was a very bad thing indeed. The "Knot Yet" report cited statistics showing that unmarried people drank more alcohol and reported being less satisfied with their lives than married people. It brought up the usual findings about children born out of wedlock experiencing more emotional instability and more problems in school than kids with married parents. It did not devote even one syllable to the subject of gay marriage.

The other writer from L.A., who I won't name even though you could figure out who she is on Google in two seconds, was the author of a bestselling book enjoining marriage-seeking women to set aside their pickiness and "settle" for men who don't necessarily meet every item on their towering list of requirements. The basis of her book had been a long article she'd published in a major national magazine. She'd taken some flak for her article, not least of all from me in my newspaper column. Admittedly, there were probably more pressing topics in the news that week for me to tackle and admittedly there was nothing inherently offensive about the author's premise in and of itself, which is that some women overlook men who'd make good husbands and fathers simply because those men aren't rich, tall, or graduates of the Ivy League. Still, with sentences on the order of "Every woman I know—no matter how successful and ambitious, how financially and emotionally secure—feels panic, occasionally coupled with desperation, if she hits thirty and finds herself unmarried" and "All I can say is, if you say you're not worried, either you're in denial or you're lying," I could no more have kept myself from smacking her down than I could have kept myself from squeezing an enormous, ripe pimple on my chin.

I'd actually known the author for years. I put us in the category of "friendly acquaintances." Or at least we'd been friendly until I took her to task in my column for setting age thirty as a sell-by date and thereby assuming that all women, no matter how successful and ambitious and secure, want marriage and children above all else. In retrospect, I see that my response was a bit off point. The article wasn't talking about people like me, who, at age thirty, happily embarked on the "adventure" of living in a lopsided, shacklike farmhouse in the rural Midwest with a guy who was about as marriageable as an electric fence. It was talking about normal people who wanted normal things. It was talking about people who get their adventuring out of the way in college or even in high school by partying so hard that by their early twenties they just want to sit on the couch watching TV with the same person for the next sixty years. It was talking about the fear and heartbreak of not finding that person as time goes on and about the realities of biological clocks. Unsurprisingly, the article was eventually expanded into the aforementioned bestselling book and the author became a therapist and highly paid speaker and life coach.

You could see why the author was a highly paid speaker; she was a damn good one. I knew this from watching her on *The Today Show* and hearing her on National Public Radio debating, for instance, another lady writer who'd published a long article about her work-life balance in the same magazine and also scored a massive book deal from it. So good a speaker was the bestselling author and so irritating and spurious was the "Knot Yet" report that I spent many, many hours preparing my presentation. I wanted to earn my $2,500 in good faith and I also wanted to make a meaningful connection with the audience, which I'd been told would be a large crowd of varying ages and political and religious persuasions from Los Angeles's well-heeled west side.

It is typical of my work pattern to devote the most time and effort to projects that have the smallest audiences and pay the least money. This is especially true of public-speaking situations, where my fear of walking up to a podium with less than three times the amount of material I need to fill the allotted time outweighs my commonsense knowledge that I'm hardly being paid anything and that very few people will show up. I once spent months preparing a lecture on "journaling" that I was asked to give as part of a wellness outreach program run by the general hospital in Lincoln, Nebraska. I pored over the diaries of Simone de Beauvoir and Virginia Woolf and Lewis and Clark. I mounted a big argument for "the journal as the fieldwork of the unconscious" and gave pointers for keeping journals that "aren't merely self-reflective but serve as a springboard for inquiry into the outside world."

I rambled on like this for forty minutes until, during the question-and-answer period, people started asking which had better deals on leather-bound diaries, Barnes and Noble or the local stationers. They asked for advice on what to do if someone reads your diary and then becomes angry with you. I was paid U.S. $0.00 for this presentation, which was appropriate because that's about how much value I added to the wellness outreach program. I told myself (and, indeed, had taken the gig because I believed) that I could use the lecture again, maybe even turning it into something that I could deliver on college campuses for generous fees. This is what I tell myself every time I agree to give a lecture, even if the lecture is tailored so specifically to the occasion (see: "Mary McCarthy at Vassar: A Centennial Celebration") that I might as well drop my one and only copy of the speech into a recycling bin as I exit the auditorium. I tell myself that it's okay that I have spent four months researching, writing, and rehearsing this speech because I can do it as a TED Talk someday. It's okay, I say, because someday it will go viral on Facebook and people will leave comments to the effect of "This will f*cking blow your mind" and "OMG: genius!"

And so it went with my fifteen-minute response to the "Knot Yet" report, a response born of my "personal mythology," which in turn was born of my family mythology. I guess the operative word here is *mythology*. The values and assumptions I'm about to describe are grievously limited in what they suggest about the wrong and right ways to live a life. Nonetheless, they are the values I grew up with and the ones that still shape my attitudes and judgments and reactions. I am ruled by them even though I no longer fully believe them, which I guess is to say that even though I can see the folly of imposing them on others, there's never going to be a day of my life that I don't breathe them in and out like oxygen itself.

The basic rundown is this. Thanks to some combination of class, generation, personal baggage, and innate temperament, my parents raised my brother and me to believe that relationships (at least the romantically and/or legally partnered kind) were for the weak. Time-consuming, physically and emotionally risky, and total nonstarters in the way of résumé building or the accumulation of A.P. credits, they were little more than distractions from the Big Life Project that was work. And though "work" tended to be murkily defined in our household (as it happened, there weren't a whole lot of A.P. credits flying around), it was clear that its opposite—domestic life, family life, the kind of life where adult concerns and interests are perpetually subsumed by a tide of parent-teacher conferences and sticky surfaces and meltdowns in the toy aisle—put a major cramp in any thinking person's style and should be put off as long as possible if not avoided entirely. That my parents were themselves living such a life—in the suburbs, no less—was a stinging irony I fully absorbed only later.

Every December, a pile of Christmas cards accumulated in a basket in the dining room. They were from faraway relatives and people my parents had known in previous lives. Many contained portrait-studio family photos or newsletters bragging about various accomplishments and/or lamenting various medical ailments. These missives were read and commented upon in depth by my parents, often with the derisive implication that if winning a Little League trophy was big-enough news to make the annual Christmas letter, this family must not have accomplished a whole lot else. But of all the nonachievements presented, none were subject to more scorn than the news that someone was getting married, especially if that person was in some way deemed too young, too nascent in his or her career, too undeveloped as a person to withstand the identity-erasing effects of formally attaching yourself to another (possibly similarly undeveloped) person.

"Jackie Harris is getting *married*," my mother would say. She would say this in the same tone as she might say *Jackie Harris got a tattoo*. Or *Jackie Harris has dropped out of that applied physics Ph.D. program and enrolled in beauty school.*

Translation: Early marriage is for the unambitious. Successful people stay single for a long time and when they've achieved everything they possibly can on their own they marry equally if not more successful people. Then their weddings are announced in *The New York Times.* Translation: If you are not important or successful enough to get your wedding announced in *The New York Times* you're not ready to get married.

·

The "Knot Yet" debate was in April. The invitation to participate had come in December. Two weeks before the event, there was still no venue. One week before the event, I was told that it would take place at a Modern Orthodox synagogue in Beverly Hills. Two days before the event, a phone conference was held among the participants, at which time the Marriage Project director asked if it was too late to do any publicity or advertising. The rabbi who led the synagogue was also on the phone and said that he would put a notice on the website and alert the members of the shul's singles' group. The Marriage Project director said he anticipated there could be as many as five hundred people in attendance and the rabbi said there was a larger auditorium we could use if the numbers exceeded the capacity of the hall we'd originally planned on.

When I arrived at the synagogue on the evening of the event, ten minutes before the start time, there was exactly one person in the audience. He was maybe fortyish, skinny and pale and crowned with a yarmulke that was attached to his balding head with painful-looking pins. He was surrounded by no fewer than seventy-four empty chairs. At the back of the room was a table with Chips Ahoy cookies and a large-capacity coffee percolator.

I thought to myself that perhaps the thing would be canceled if no one else showed up. Years ago, on a book tour, I'd arrived at a bookstore in Saint Paul, Minnesota, to find that exactly one person had come to my reading. It seemed that David Sedaris was doing a reading and book signing at the university that very same night, thereby tapping every single literary-minded person in the region and effectively making my reading the equivalent of a barely known sitcom competing with the number-one-rated show airing at the same time on another network. The person who had come turned out to be a big fan. She was a very young woman living on her parents' farm in rural Minnesota and she'd driven an hour to see me. It was obvious that the only decent thing to do was to take her to see David Sedaris. So we got ourselves over to the university, where Sedaris's talk was so packed we had to watch him on a Jumbotron.

Just as I was wondering if the Marriage Project would still pay me if we canceled the show and offered to take our sole audience member to the alternate cultural event of his choice (which he would surely refuse, thereby freeing me to go home), more attendees began trickling in. There was an elderly couple and a young, twenty-something couple and a gaggle of women-of-a-certain-age whose slightly provocative attire (a leopard-print blouse here, a sequined top there) suggested this might be some kind of girls' night out. At least half the women in the audience, which was now numbering into the low double digits, wore wigs or some other kind of head covering. At least a quarter of the entire audience, presumably members of the singles' group, looked like they might be pushing fifty. There were patchy mustaches and ill-fitting electric-blue sweaters that could only have been purchased at T.J. Maxx by septuagenarian mothers holding out hope that their future daughter-in-law was just a J-Date away.

I took my place at the table next to the bestselling author and the rabbi introduced us. The Marriage Project director went to the podium and reported his findings on "rates of marriage satisfaction." He also talked about how television programs like *Sex and the City* glorified the single life in ultimately damaging ways. Next came the second report author, who said that most people mistakenly believe that physical attraction is the first thing to look for in a partner, when in fact research has shown that the happiest marriages are those in which sexual chemistry arises only after basic compatibility is established. The audience was attentive, if not rapt. By the time I approached the podium, I felt confident that I'd win the evening, even though the bestselling writer was speaking last. I thanked the Marriage Project guys for inviting me and the rabbi for hosting us. Then I fired up my ignition.

I started out by saying that I was glad to see that a conversation about a "trend" was finally addressing the ways in which that trend affected the nonelite classes as well as the wine-sipping, *New York Times* Style-section-reading demographic that usually provides the fodder for grand pronouncements about social phenomena. I talked about how there was truth in the assertion that "Middle Americans" were often putting the baby before the bridal shower—or skipping marriage altogether—but that the reasons were likely more rooted in economics than in a desire to emulate the characters on *Sex and the City*. I talked about how the demise of manufacturing jobs has meant many working-class and lower-class women are the breadwinners in their families and therefore lack the financial incentive to commit to a male partner. I then shifted course slightly and spoke about the way five- and six-figure price tags on weddings and the fetishization of gift registries and lavish honeymoons and bridal paraphernalia had made marriage seem less like the ultimate life choice than the ultimate life*style*. I suggested that if our chief cultural images of marriage are dominated by consumer fantasies, not least of all setting up a household filled with magazine-ready decor and "grown-up furniture," it should be no shock that less-affluent people are skipping that step altogether.

"In other words," I said, "if we're going to talk about socioeconomic divides in marriage trends, we'd do well to think about the materialism that's endemic to our contemporary concept of marriage. When the average wedding in America costs thirty thousand dollars and there are entire cable channels that seemingly place a higher premium on finding the right dress than finding the right partner, why should we be surprised that the less affluent are seeing it as less than essential?"

I was kicking major ass, clearly. What a lively social critique! What a potent cocktail of insight and indignation (with a light garnish of sanctimony)! Though the audience registered no more expression than it had during the first two speakers, which is to say practically none, I told myself that it was probably out of politeness. Maybe Orthodox Jews were more like New England WASPs than was commonly imagined. Maybe they were thoroughly engaged and amused but too uptight or inadequately plied with gin to actually laugh or appear interested.

I forged ahead. I picked some bones with some of the Marriage Project's research findings, much of which seemed to me to have a classic causation-versus-correlation problem. I suggested that even if it was true that unmarried people in their twenties are more likely to be depressed, drink excessively, and report lower levels of satisfaction than their married counterparts, how do we know this is because they're not married? Maybe they're not married because they're depressed. Or maybe the kinds of people who are apt to delay marriage are also the kinds apt to be depressed—or just more likely to talk about being depressed. Maybe they're more likely to occupy social spheres where people go to therapy and pick apart their psyches or go to parties and drink more than they would if they stayed home.

"Maybe people who put off getting married are more prone to a certain kind of chronic life dissatisfaction," I said. "No one's good enough, which maybe has something to do with why they're alone. In other words, maybe being happy or unhappy might not have to do with being married as much as, simply, being the person we are."

I took a drink of water. I was starting to get a little choked up. The audience still appeared unmoved but I felt confident I was just seconds away from delivering a major aha moment.

"Sure," I said, "there are cultural forces out there that can cause people to walk away from fantastic relationships because, as the 'Knot Yet' report suggests, they don't yet feel they have their ducks in a row. As the next speaker will probably tell you, it's not even about the row of ducks but about shallow requirements that cause us to reject people for reasons that ultimately have no bearing on what kind of partners they'll make. Sometimes it's about thinking we haven't yet become the person we want to be when we meet the right person. It's about having some fantasy version of a perfect self and the perfect mate that self will attract. But sometimes it's really much simpler and more boring than that. Sometimes it's because we just haven't met the right person yet. Sometimes it's because that person comes along not during high school or college or during that summer lifeguarding job but during your thirties or even your forties or fifties."

And, finally, my pièce de résistance:

"As fun as it is to look at graphs and pie charts and Venn diagrams showing why we make the decisions we do," I said, "the fact is that the human heart is pretty pie chart resistant."

It was such a good line I was almost embarrassed. I was embarrassed for the Marriage Project guys, with their Power-Point and the weird way, despite sounding like therapists on a Christian call-in radio show, they stepped around any mention of their religious orientation. Mostly, though, I was embarrassed for the bestselling author. Skilled speaker though she was, there was no way in hell her remarks were going to compete with mine. She was droll and appealing, but she was canned. She purported to be a truth teller but she was really a provocateur, a saleswoman, a brand. She may have sold more books than I ever had or would but the real truth teller here was me. If even just one member of the audience, perhaps a leopard-print-blouse-wearing member of the singles' group, walked out of that synagogue thinking, *Hey, my heart is not a pie chart*, I'd consider it a job well done. Lip quivering in anticipation of my own profundity, I brought it on home.

"Choosing a partner wisely involves logic and rationality, of course, but it also involves that woefully unscientific method called 'just knowing,'" I said. "And some people *just know* in their twenties and others don't know until much later. And that is why ultimately this discussion, fascinating as it is in many ways, is, to me, only as useful as our ability to accept the randomness of life. To think not in terms of 'I must marry by twenty or thirty or forty' but 'I must respect the life and the timeline I was given and live with authenticity as well as compassion and commitment.'"

The crowd sat there, jaws as slack as they'd been at the beginning. They applauded respectfully.

The bestselling author stepped up to the podium. "I feel like I'm going to cry," she said. "That was so romantic."

She then proceeded to bring the house down by reading from the introduction to her book. It was centered on an analogy for female pickiness she'd called the Husband Store. There were six floors in the Husband Store and you could only visit the place one time. The first floor offered men who had good jobs. If that wasn't enough, women could proceed to the second floor, which carried men who had good jobs and loved kids. The goods grew increasingly fine (men who have good jobs, love kids, help equally with housework, give back rubs, et cetera) until the sixth floor, where women were told that there were no men on that floor and that the showroom existed only to show that women were impossible to please. "Thank you for shopping the Husband Store," they were told.

The audience roared with laughter. They slapped their knees and leaned forward so as not to miss a word. They rocked back and forth in their seats, as though davening to the ghost of Henny Youngman. The single women smiled big, toothy, happy smiles. The extremely pale guy in the yarmulke nodded in recognition. Next to me, the "Knot Yet" authors chuckled in appreciation, seemingly unperturbed that the speaker was making no reference whatsoever to their report.

We had all taken so long with our remarks that there were only about five minutes left for the "debate" and questions from the audience. Most of the questions were for the bestselling author. What did she think of online dating? Did she recommend using a private matchmaker? An elderly man with a cane stood up and thanked her for her humor and perspective.

"Obviously, you're the practical one and Meghan is the romantic one," he said.

I had never once in my life been called romantic. At least not when it came to love. Unrealistic, yes. Maybe hopeful, myopic, "trying too hard to control the narrative" (there's a typical Husband Store shopper trait for you). But romantic? I would probably sooner be called mushy or moony, which would never happen because I have never been these things (except for around dogs, which is an entirely separate issue). Delivering my talk, especially this talk, and then being called a romantic felt akin to showing up to the polls and voting for one political party and then returning to my car to find that someone had slapped on a bumper sticker advertising the other. I felt misunderstood to the point of feeling violated. The rabbi wrapped up the Q&A and reminded everyone that the bestselling author would be signing and selling books in the back.

As the audience filed out, the man with the cane approached me.

"I think you're the first person to ever call me a romantic," I told him.

"Well, you're certainly not practical," he said.

I paused for a moment. He had not said this unkindly.

"I guess I was talking about living authentically," I said.

"But isn't that the same as living romantically?"

Shortly before my mother left my father, right around their twenty-fifth wedding anniversary, she told me one of the things that had kept her hanging on in recent years was her desire to emulate a General Electric commercial that showed an elderly couple in their darkened kitchen, dancing to the light of the open refrigerator. "I want someone who will dance with me in the refrigerator light," she said. I noted that this was a very different statement than saying she wanted to be married to my father for another twenty-five years, given his aversion to both dancing and wasting power.

Still, it was hard to begrudge her this momentary dip into corporate-sponsored tear jerking. I, too, had a history of taking television ads a little too much to heart. Around that time I was consistently moved by an ad for New York Telephone. It opened with a young couple arguing in the doorway of their apartment, the man yelling, "I'm gone," as he tugs on his blazer and dashes in a huff down the steps of their Manhattan brownstone. After a montage showing New Yorkers of all walks of life answering their ringing phones and brimming with ecstasy at the sounds of their loved ones' voices on the other end, the ad circles back to the couple. The man is calling from a phone booth (this was back in the days of phone booths). "I'm sorry," he says. "Come home," the woman says. The harmonizing jingle singers (this was back in the days of jingle singers) belt out the song's refrain one last time: "We're all connected."

Back when this ad was airing, I longed for the day that someone would love me enough to share a brownstone apartment from which he would storm out during an argument and call me later from a pay phone to apologize. This was my version of dancing in the refrigerator light. But just as my mother did the math and decided that another quarter century of unhappiness was not worth a three-minute waltz in the glow of a 40-watt bulb, I left New York when I needed to, even though it meant I'd probably never peer ruefully out of the bay windows as my man skulked off in a snit. Instead, I would argue with men in other places, such as hotel rooms at the Hilton Towers and apartments in Los Angeles and, more times than I'd be able to count, in moving cars in which I was either a nagging passenger or nagged-upon driver. My mother would go on to have refrigerators that stored no one's perishables but her own. Her happiness with that arrangement would more than make up for any unfulfilled dreams spawned by General Electric.

Marriage is hard work at any age; that platitude is, sadly,

as true as it is hackneyed. But now that I'm old enough to accumulate my own stack of holiday cards every year, some of them from the Jackie Harrises of the world, who were reckless enough to get married before the age of thirty but often seem to beam the brightest in their family photos (probably because they also had kids earlier and those kids are now sentient beings who will soon be capable of driving themselves to band practice), I've observed something that probably would have surprised my mother: The young are often harder workers—or at least better team players—in the quarry that is marriage. They do not, as I did, bring a mortgage and a mid-stage career and an assemblage of tastes and opinions and biases and assumptions formed over more than three decades. They bring only a toothbrush. Whatever else they need, they'll acquire as a couple. Whatever kind of people they turn out to be, they'll turn into under the heady influence of the other.

At least that's my theory. It's also the theory behind cornerstone marriage, the operative word being *theory*, since in practice there are infinite ways to wreck a marriage. I was struck, however, by the National Marriage Project's finding that after a certain point, the correlation between delayed marriage and successful marriage for the well-educated diminishes with age. That is to say, educated couples who marry in their mid- to late twenties are happier than those who marry in their teens or early twenties. But those who wait until their mid to late thirties see diminishing returns on the benefits of postponement, not least of all because of overly individualistic mind-sets—"me-ness" versus "we-ness," you could call it— and what the researchers called "relational cynicism."

As I drove home from the synagogue that night I felt as though I were inhaling a kind of vaporous, free-floating anxiety. My husband and I had been going through a strange patch. I won't say rough patch, because we'd had those and this, mercifully, did not qualify. But we were sad in ways we couldn't always admit to ourselves and needy in ways that were not always recognizable to the other. Our dog, who'd started out as *my* dog before my husband came along and pledged his devotion to us both, had recently died after months of slow, heartbreaking decline. Our house had been rendered intolerably silent in the dog's absence and we'd attempted to soothe ourselves by rescuing a new dog that we would eventually come to love but that still felt like a friend's pet we were merely looking after. We spent most nights watching a one-to-two-hour string of television, beginning with *The Daily Show* and *The Colbert Report* on Comedy Central, which we'd dubbed "the news," and ending with whatever high-end cable drama had us in its thrall.

When I got home, my husband was sitting in the desk chair I'd given him for his birthday. He was playing Scrabble on the computer. The new dog was sleeping in the old dog's bed. The rusty chandelier in the study, a poorly wired piece of quasi-chic shabbery I'd bought at a flea market, was flickering on and off. I'd hoped to make the room look like something in a crumbling French estate, but instead it was just a dim repository of books and files and random computer cords. The floor was always littered with shavings caused by an eternally jammed paper shredder. My husband asked how the debate went.

I told him that the bestselling author was a genius. She'd earned her $2,500 by preparing not a single syllable of original material. And the audience loved her for it.

"Plus, they called me a romantic," I said.

"Well, you are one, kind of," he said. "Just look at this stupid light fixture."

Is being authentic the same as being romantic? Is it a *form* of being romantic? My assumption has always been that the two are diametrically opposed. If romance connotes a certain indulgence of attractive falsehoods, authenticity is about indulging only the truth, embracing what's in front of you, working with what you have. And since authenticity has long been a major interest of mine, since it's what I'm *about*, I figured romance just wasn't part of my constitution. I thought lines like "the human heart is pretty pie chart resistant" were coming from a place of stony pragmatism rather than the foolishness of the sixth floor of the Husband Store.

But perhaps I was mistaken about myself. I may have spent a good deal of my life avoiding, if not downright fleeing from, the prospect of long-term commitment, but I did chase after experiences and also the stories I could tell about them. In some ways that's an utterly unromantic impulse, a sort of "thinking person's" guide to using people and then discarding them when their novelties have worn off. But maybe in other ways it's almost the epitome of romance—or at least the epitome of something a romantic would do. What is more dreamily reckless, after all, than dating people in part for their plotlines—the ones they bring with them and the ones we take with us when we leave? What is more fanciful than wondering, if only for the sake of perversity and if only for a fleeting moment, if a destitute mountain man or a malapropism-prone airline pilot could be the One? What is more hopeful than mistakenly thinking that a bunch of senior citizens in Nebraska want a tutorial on Simone de Beauvoir or that lonely singles need a lecture about respecting the timeline they've been given?

Not much that I can think of. Of course, these are also the sorts of things that can lead to riding in the backseat of your own car. Though, let's face it, a little time back there never hurt anyone. The view is different and you just might learn something.

NOT WHAT IT USED TO BE

My husband has been known to reminisce about his college years, often saying that the friendships he had then were deeper than any since, that his highs were higher, his disappointments more shattering, his convictions more deeply felt. Last year I finally made good on my promise (possibly it was a threat) to have us sit down and watch *The Big Chill*, the iconic 1983 movie about a group of old college friends grappling with the fact that they are no longer impassioned students but adult participants in late twentieth-century capitalism. I expected it to be painfully dated but found it to have held up far better than I'd imagined. *The Big Chill*, of course, is the godmother of *thirtysomething*, the television series about the exact same types of people worrying about the exact same things. Together they more or less defined the image of the "yuppie," a label that now feels musty and lazy but remains a template for the concept of socioeconomic upward mobility as an active, conscious gesture.

Though I was only thirteen when *The Big Chill* was released and therefore mainly interested in the soundtrack, which featured Three Dog Night's "Joy to the World" (known to my peers and me as "Jeremiah Was a Bullfrog"), *thirty-something* premiered on network television the fall of my senior year in high school, a time when my primary interest was sloughing off the residue of youth and becoming a grown-up as quickly as possible. *Thirtysomething*, true to its title, was about adults. It was about two married couples, Hope and Michael and Nancy and Elliot, and also about a handful of single people who were portrayed as some combination of earnest and quirky but were usually looked down upon as immature and neurotic. The married adults with kids on the show were engaged in the "juggling act" (a national pastime in the '80s) of raising young children and advancing their careers and in one case restoring their charming Craftsman house. The single ones were interesting and impassioned but also possessed of some flaw—workaholism, insecurity, authority issues—that made them their "own worst enemies." Many frequently wore sweatshirts bearing the names of their colleges and, like *The Big Chill* characters, often wondered aloud what had happened to their younger, more hopeful selves. Because it was a television show they were all great-looking and dressed really well, though because it was the late 1980s many of the sweaters had ugly geometric patterns and the women's suits had huge shoulder pads.

Most of us have unconscious disbeliefs about our lives, facts that we accept at face value but that still cause us to gasp just a little when they pass through our minds at certain angles. Mine are these: that my mother is dead, that the Vatican actually had it in itself to select a pope like Pope Francis, and that I am now older than the characters on *thirtysomething*. That last one is especially upending. How is it that the people who were, for me, the very embodiment of adulthood, who, with their dinner parties and marital spats and career angst represented *the place in life I'd like to get to but surely never will*, are on average six to eight years my junior? How did I get to be middle-aged without actually growing up?

Luckily, even some of the most confounding questions have soothingly prosaic answers. On the subject of growing up, or feeling that you have succeeded in doing so, I'm pretty sure the consensus is that it's an illusion. Probably no one ever really feels grown-up, except for certain high school math teachers or members of Congress. I suspect that most members of AARP go around feeling in many ways just as confused and fraudulent as most middle school students. You might even be able to make a case that not feeling grown-up is a sign that you actually *are*, much as worrying that you're crazy supposedly means you're not.

My husband gave *The Big Chill* a B minus. He said he would have given it a C minus if not for Meg Tilly, who spent most of the movie in a leotard and tights, contorting her exceptionally lithe body into positions not possible for most human anatomies. He said the film struck him as a bunch of old people complaining.

"The characters are younger than we are," I said.

"No they're not," my husband said.

"Yes they are," I said. "They're supposed to have graduated from the University of Michigan fifteen years earlier."

"So?"

"We graduated twenty-one years ago."

My husband is nostalgic for his college days. I, on the other hand, spent most of college waiting for it to be over so I could move to the city and work at an entry-level office job. Believe me, I know how lame that sounds. Among my greatest sources of opprobrium and regret is that I managed to have such a mediocre time at a place that is pretty much custom designed for delivering the best years of your life. I'd like to say that I wasn't the same person back then that I later became and now am. But the truth is that I was the exact same person. I was more myself then than at any other time in my life. I was an extreme version of myself. Everything I've always felt I felt more intensely. Everything I've always wanted, I wanted more. Everything I currently dislike, I downright *hated* back then. People who think I'm judgmental, impatient, and obsessed with real estate now should have seen me in college. I was bored by many of my classmates and irked by the contrived mischief and floundering sexual intrigues of dormitory life. I couldn't wait to get out and rent my own apartment, preferably one in a grand Edwardian building on the Upper West Side of Manhattan. In that sense, I guess my college experience was just as intense as my husband's. I just view that intensity negatively rather than nostalgically, which perhaps is its own form of nostalgia.

A little game I like to play is to look back on various critical junctures in my life and imagine what advice my older self might dispense to my younger self. The way I picture it, my younger self will be going about her business and my older self will suddenly appear out of nowhere, like a goon sent in to settle a debt. I always imagine my older self grabbing my younger self by the collar or even shoving her in some manner. At first, Younger Self is frightened and irritated (Older Self speaks harshly to her) but a feeling of calm quickly sets in over the encounter. Younger Self sits there rapt, as though receiving the wisdom of Yoda or of some musician she idolizes, such as Joni Mitchell. But Older Self is no Yoda. Older Self is stern and sharp. Older Self has adopted the emphatic, no-nonsense speaking style of formidable women with whom she worked in countless New York City offices before deciding she never again wanted to work anywhere but her own home (a place where, over the years, she has lost a certain amount of people skills and has been known to begin conversations as though slamming a cleaver into a side of raw beef). Older Self begins her sentences with "Listen" and "Look." She says, "Listen, what you're into right now isn't working for you." She says, "Look, do yourself a favor and get out of this situation right now. All of it. The whole situation. Leave this college. Forget about this boy you're sleeping with but not actually dating. Stop pretending you did the reading for your Chaucer seminar when you didn't and never will."

To which Younger Self will ask, "Okay, then what should I do?" And of course Older Self has no answer, because Older Self did not leave the college, did not drop the boy, did not stop pretending to have read Chaucer. And the cumulative effect of all those failures (or missed opportunities, blown chances, fuckups, whatever) is sitting right here, administering a tongue-lashing to her younger self (which is to say *her*self) about actions or inactions that were never going to be anything other than what they were. And at that point the younger and older selves merge into some kind of floating blob of unfortunate yet inevitable life choices, at which point I stop the little game and nudge my mind back into real time and try to think about other things, such as what I might have for dinner that night or what might happen when I die. Such is the pendulum of my post-forty thoughts.

·

Once upon a time, in the early 1990s, my generation was the cohort people were interested in. It had been dubbed Generation X, thanks to a novel of the same name by a later-born boomer named Douglas Coupland. As a term, it was sexy. It sold magazines and launched MTV's *Real World* franchise, which, as I write this, is in its twenty-ninth season, though I've missed the last twenty-six of them. But by the mid-aughts, Generation X was a passing thought, a low-budget indie movie sandwiched between two blockbusters known as the baby boomers and the children of the baby boomers, who are known as the millennials. By most counts there are something like 78 million boomers and 76 million millennials. There are 51 million Gen Xers. As a demographic, we're a minor player. No one cares all that much about our spending habits or voting patterns. Chapter four of Coupland's novel is entitled "I Am Not a Target Market." How right he was.

The default posture of Generation X has always been to trash the boomers. The boomers were yuppie sellouts, sanctimonious blowhards, fair-weather hippies who joined the establishment as soon as they realized the upsides to having health insurance and retirement accounts (see: backstories of *Big Chill* characters and Hope and Michael et al.). They did tons of drugs and had tons of sex and then left us to trudge through the AIDS and crack epidemics they left in their wake. If you were a young writer in the 1990s, as I was, you could find a steady stream of magazine work composing irony-laden rants about how much the boomers had screwed over the Xers—economically, culturally, sexually-transmitted-diseasedly, et cetera. In the span of a few years, I wrote no fewer than fifteen articles that were essentially some variation on "broken homes ruined our belief in marriage, MTV ruined our attention spans, and AIDS ruined our sex lives. Our world and the baby boomers' world are many galaxies apart."

Twenty years later, I see that this is utterly untrue. Generation Xers and baby boomers have nearly everything in common. At least, just about everything that means anything, like reading actual books or enjoying face-to-face contact with friends and not necessarily wanting to watch a movie on a three-and-a-half-inch screen. The vagaries of the digital revolution mean that I have more in common with people twenty years my senior than I do with people seven years my junior. Some of my best friends are baby boomers. Far fewer are millennials.

In 1994, the anchors of NBC's *Today Show* had an off-air conversation that would become as powerful a lens as any through which to view the vast gulf between those who came of age before the Internet era and those who've never known anything else. It took place with cameras rolling, presumably during a commercial break or prerecorded segment, and resurfaced in the form of a YouTube video seventeen years later. The video shows the anchors Katie Couric, Bryant Gumbel, and Elizabeth Vargas responding to Gumbel's confusion over how to narrate a title card that reads "violence@ nbc.ge."

The transcript (picture Couric with asymmetrical haircut and in dowdy cardigan; picture Vargas looking oddly like the mom from *The Cosby Show*; picture Gumbel looking, as ever, like an impatient driver just cut off in traffic) is as follows:

> Gumbel: I wasn't prepared to translate that. As I was doing that little tease. That little mark with the "a" and the ring around it?

Vargas: "At"?

Gumbel: See, that's what I said.

Vargas: Um-hmm.

Gumbel: Katie said she thought it was "about."

Couric: Yeah. Or "around."

Vargas: Oh.

Gumbel: But I'd never heard it said [out loud].

Couric: Yeah.

Gumbel: I'd seen the mark but never heard it said and then it sounded stupid when I said it. Violence at nbcge com. I mean . . .

Couric: Well, Allison should know—

Gumbel: What is Internet, anyway?

Couric: Internet is that massive computer network.

Vargas: Right.

Couric: The one that's becoming really big now.

Gumbel: What do you mean, it's big? How do you mean? Do you write to it? Like mail?

Couric: No, a lot of people use it . . . I guess they can communicate with NBC, writers and producers. [Calling to someone offscreen] Allison, can you explain what Internet is?

Gumbel: No, she can't say anything in ten seconds or less.

Vargas: Uh-oh! Allison will be in the studio shortly.

Couric: What does it mean?

Male voice offscreen: It's a giant computer network made up of, uh . . . started from—

Gumbel: Oh, I thought you were going to tell us what this [makes @ symbol with finger] means.

Vargas: It's like a computer billboard.

Male voice offscreen: It's a computer billboard.

Vargas: Right.

Male voice offscreen: It has several universities that are all joined together.

Vargas: Right.

Gumbel: And others can access it?

Male voice offscreen: And it's getting bigger and bigger all the time.

Vargas: Right.

Gumbel: Just great.

Vargas: It came in really handy during the quake. A lot of people, that's how they were communicating out to tell family and loved ones they were okay because all the phone lines were down.

Gumbel: I was telling Katie the other—

Couric: But you don't need a phone line to operate Internet?

Vargas: No. No, apparently not.

I was twenty-four when this conversation took place, a full-grown adult by most measures. The exchange, while quaint and amusing, doesn't surprise me or seem strange in any way. That's because even though various incipient forms of digital communication had by then been going on for decades, I, like most people, was similarly ignorant about "Internet." Like Katie Couric, I was a creature of telephone landlines. Like Bryant Gumbel, who, unless I'm mistaken, appears to be rolling his eyes when he deems these rapid advancements "just great," I was, if not *suspicious* of technology, at least left a bit cold by it. Couric and Gumbel, both bona fide boomers, are fourteen years and twenty-two years older than I am, respectively. But as a Gen Xer, my sensibility is more closely aligned with theirs than with that of a lot of people born just five or six years after me. That's be-cause the digital revolution has installed a sense of "before" and "after" that's as palpable as any war, any catastrophe, maybe even any coming and going of a messiah. And any millen-nial can see that any Gen Xer, no matter how tech savvy or early adaptive, belongs to the group of those who came before.

A thirteen-year-old I know has a habit of phoning people repeatedly and hanging up when no one answers. Thanks to caller ID, he does not understand the concept of leaving a message. "You can see that I called you," he says to me. "That's how you know to call me back." I tell him that seeing that someone phoned isn't enough, that we need to know what they want and where and when to return the call. I tell him that leaving phone messages is an important skill and that, if he likes, he can practice by leaving some for me. He looks at me like I'm suggesting he learn how to operate a cotton gin. To try to explain to a thirteen-year-old the im-portance of leaving a callback number is essentially to bathe yourself in a sepia tint. You might as well be an old-timey portrait in a Ken Burns documentary, fading in and out be-tween stock photos of drum-cylinder printing presses while Patricia Clarkson reads from your letters. By the time this boy is twenty, there may well be no more voice mail. By the time he is thirty there may be no more desktop computers. By the time he is forty, scientists may have learned how to reprogram human biology to turn off genes that cause aging and disease. By then I will be seventy. It will be too late to turn off my genes. It will be too late for a lot of things. Maybe not to travel or to try, again, to read Chaucer but definitely too late to assume any role that's preceded by the word *young.* It's already too late for that. Any traces of precocity I ever had are long forgotten. I am not and will never again be a young writer, a young homeowner, a young teacher. I was never a young wife. The only thing I could do now for which my youth would be a truly notable feature would be to die. If I died now, I'd die young. Everything else, I'm doing middle-aged.

I am nostalgic for my twenties (most of them, anyway; twenty and twenty-one were squandered at college; twenty-four was kind of a wash, too) but I can tell you for sure that they weren't as great as I now crack them up to be. I was always broke, I was often lonely, and I had some really terrible clothes. But my life was shiny and unblemished. Everything was ahead of me. I walked around with an abiding feeling that, at any given time, anything could go in any direction. And it was often true. In the same way that, for the first few weeks of my first year of college, an errant stroll down the hall of any dormitory might lead to an invitation to come into some-one's room and talk about some indie band, after which my body almost seemed to convulse from the electrical surges of "making a real connection," I found my twenties to be a time of continual surprise. I would leave a party in a brownstone apartment, hear another party behind the door of an-other apartment on the way down the narrow stairs, and decide I had enough wind left in my sails to walk on in. I didn't want to miss anything. I wanted to stretch out over the city like a giant octopus. I wanted enough appendages to be able to ring every door buzzer simultaneously. There was some switch turned on in my brain that managed to make 90 percent of conversations feel interesting or useful or, if nothing else, worth referencing later if only by way of describing how *boring* this person was who I got stuck talking to.

Or at least it's easy to remember it that way. Probably I was far less of a bon vivant than all that. Probably the reason I ducked into strange parties was that I'd failed to meet anyone of potential romantic interest at the first one and thought there might be a few more stones to turn over at the second. Probably I actually barely crashed any parties at all. Probably the sum total over the entire decade was two or three. Probably the fact that they were such rare occurrences is the very thing that makes me remember them as a regular habit. Novelty has a way of intensifying memory. The less often you do something, the deeper the memory burrows in. I remember that at one of the parties I wandered into there were two Old English sheepdogs milling around the packed living room. I don't recall if I talked to any people but I do know that I knelt down and hugged one of those dogs as if its softness and warm, drooly breath were the only things that would give me the strength to walk home. This was a time in my life when I was so filled with longing for so many things that were so far out of reach that at least once a day I thought my heart would implode from the sheer force of unrequited desire.

By *desire* I am not referring to apartments I wanted to occupy or furniture I wanted to buy or even people I was attracted to (well, I'm referring to those things a little) but, rather, a sensation I can only describe as the ache of not being there yet. If my older self had descended upon my twenty-something self and informed her that she'd spend the next several decades reminiscing about this time in her life, the twenty-something self would have been more than a little disconcerted, possibly even devastated. I can imagine her looking at Older Self in horrified astonishment. "I'm going to be reminiscing about *this*?" she'd ask while the ATM spat out her card and flashed "insufficient funds" across the screen. "You're telling me that when I'm forty-five I'll be pining for the temp jobs and cheap shoes that now comprise my life? You're telling me this is as good as it gets? You're telling me, contrary to everything I tell myself, that it's actually all *down*hill from here?"

To which I'd hope that Older Self would have the good sense to assure Younger Self that that is not what she is saying, that indeed things will only go up from here. Maybe not right away and certainly not without some deep valleys to offset the peaks (as well as a few sharp left turns, as long as we're speaking in euphemisms) but with enough steadiness to suggest that whatever she is doing now more or less constitutes being on the right track.

"Listen," Older Self might say. "The things that right now seem permanently out of reach, you'll reach them eventually. You'll have a career, a house, a partner in life. You will have much better shoes. You will reach a point where your funds will generally be sufficient—maybe not always plentiful, but sufficient."

But here's what Older Self will not have the heart to say: some of the music you are now listening to—the CDs you play while you stare out the window and think about the five million different ways your life might go—will be unbearable to listen to in twenty years. They will be unbearable not because they will sound dated and trite but because they will sound like the lining of your soul. They will take you straight back to the place you were in when you felt that anything could happen at any time, that your life was a huge room with a thousand doors, that your future was not only infinite but also elastic. They will be unbearable because they will remind you that at least half of the things you once planned for your future are now in the past and others got reabsorbed into your imagination before you could even think about acting on them. It will be as though you'd never thought of them in the first place, as if they were never meant to be anything more than passing thoughts you had while playing your stereo at night.

The records I cannot listen to today without returning to that feeling of imminent heart implosion include Suzanne Vega's 1985 eponymous debut album and Jeff Buckley's 1994 debut (and final, it turned out) album, *Grace*. Specifically, the second track on the Suzanne Vega album, a slightly discordant, wintry song called "Freeze Tag," and "So Real," the fifth track on *Grace*, which was dark and loud and spoke of the smell of couch fabric and a "simple city dress" in a way that made me feel like New York City itself had backed me up against the wall of some dive bar after seducing me into a state of vertigo.

It's interesting that these records come nearly a decade apart. When I discovered Suzanne Vega I was a senior in high school. My parents' marriage was in the early stages of disintegration. I had recently come into an understanding that New York City, which was a thirty-minute ride away by New Jersey Transit but might as well have been across the international date line, was a place where people actually lived. My adolescence was now split into a before and an after: the time before I knew I had to live in New York City and the time after. The combination of knowing this and not being able to do anything about it was excruciating. Life was now a way station between the constraints of childhood and the endless horizon of adulthood. I remember sitting in homeroom before the morning bell, listening to "Freeze Tag" on my Sony Walkman and nearly shaking with excitement at the thought of the day when I'd pay my own bills, secure my own meals, make mistakes without my parents watching.

The lyrics bore no direct relationship to these thoughts. They painted a scene of a chilly playground where "the sun is fading fast upon the slides into the past." They told of "swings of indecision" and of only being able to "say yes." Maybe it was the song's spirit of limitlessness that drew me in. Very soon, I told myself, I would embark on a life in which there was time for a hundred different versions of myself. I would go through countless phases, have more iterations and incarnations than I could possibly imagine. I would know everyone and live everywhere. I would use every crayon in the box. I would be the youngest person in the room for a very long time.

The Jeff Buckley album came over my transom when I was twenty-five, one year after it was released. (Two years later, Buckley, at age thirty, would drown in an inlet of the Mississippi River near Memphis.) Twenty-five was a big year for me, a painful, wonderful, deeply necessary year. I ended a long relationship with a man who wanted to get married and have children. I bleached my hair white, dated some men I shouldn't have, tried in vain to be a lesbian, and could feel the engines of my career quietly revving up beneath me. I took a bartending class. I tried waitressing at a jazz club. I took exactly four guitar lessons and one modern dance class. In all cases, I either proved myself hopelessly inept or simply lacking in the patience necessary to develop any level of

proficiency, so I gave up and went back to writing and working temp jobs in offices. I couldn't afford taxis but sometimes
took them anyway. I got deeply into debt but believed I would
get out of it eventually. A time would come when I would
stop believing this, but, at twenty-five, the debt was a fresh
wound that still had the potential to heal without a scar. I lay
on my bed and listened to "So Real" and thought that I was
mere inches away from being the person I wanted to be. My
fingertips could almost touch that person. That person was
both very specific (respected essayist, resident of the 10025
zip code, lover of large, long-haired dogs) and someone who
took multiple forms, who could go in any direction, who
might be a bartender or a guitar player or a lesbian or a modern dancer or an office temp on Sixth Avenue. That person
was still usually the youngest person in the room.

Now that I am almost never the youngest person in any
room I realize that what I miss most about those times is the
very thing that drove me so mad back when I was living in
them. What I miss is the feeling that nothing has started yet,
that the future towers over the past, that the present is merely
a planning phase for the gleaming architecture that will
make up the skyline of the rest of my life. But what I forget is
the loneliness of all that. If everything is ahead then nothing
is behind. You have no ballast. You have no tailwinds either.
You hardly ever know what to do, because you've hardly
done anything. I guess this is why wisdom is supposed to be
the consolation prize of aging. It's supposed to give us better
things to do than stand around and watch in disbelief as the
past casts long shadows over the future.

The problem, I now know, is that no one ever really feels
wise, least of all those who actually have it in themselves to
be so. The Older Self of our imagination never quite folds

itself into the older self we actually become. Instead, it hovers in the perpetual distance like a highway mirage. It's the destination that never gets any closer even as our life histories pile up behind us in the rearview mirror. It is the reason that I got to forty-something without ever feeling thirty-something. It is why I hope that if I make it to eighty-something I have the good sense not to pull out those old CDs. My heart, by then, surely would not be able to keep from imploding. My heart, back then, stayed in one piece only because, as bursting with anticipation as it was, it had not yet been strained by nostalgia. It had not yet figured out that life is mostly an exercise in being something other than what we used to be while remaining fundamentally—and sometimes maddeningly—who we are.

HONORARY DYKE

There was a period in my life, roughly between the ages of thirty-two and thirty-five, when pretty much anyone who saw me would have assumed I was a lesbian. I had very short, almost spiky hair, owned three pairs of Chuck Taylor tennis shoes, and wore lots of cargo pants with tank tops and silver jewelry. (That was my casual wear; for dressier occasions I'd taken to almost exclusively wearing cheongsams with ballet flats.) I had a toe ring. I drove a Subaru station wagon— mint green, manual transmission, metal dog gate behind the backseat. (That's not to imply that there's anything especially lesbionic about mint green, though stick shifts and dog gates do emit a certain undeniable Sapphic energy.) As for the dog himself, I took him to coffee shops with outdoor seating and to independent bookstores, which always seem to allow dogs. At night, he slept in my bed, his 85 pounds of fur and flesh and drool crowding me to the edge. He was effectively my boyfriend, but I probably would have been better off with a real boyfriend. For instance, someone who would take me out to dinner and do boyfriendy things like tell me that my car needed a new timing belt. But I attracted no suitable

candidates. I was essentially a soft butch. The only man likely
to approach me would have been one who needed directions
to the Dinah Shore Weekend in Palm Springs.

The weird part was that I knew what I was doing. I had
a distinct look in mind. My desired vibe was androgynous
yet enticing; earthy yet sporty with a hint of punk rock; Smith
College meets East Village circa 1985. I was going for a
chick singer-songwriter kind of thing. I wanted the sharp,
angular haircut of Shawn Colvin on the cover of her 1989
debut album, *Steady On*. I wanted to look like one of my all-
time musical heroes, the gifted and underrecognized Jona-
tha Brooke, who had supershort hair for much of her career
but managed to offset any overtly butch undertones by wearing things like velvet pants and halter tops with about five
different necklaces.

The problem was that I didn't really have the raw mate-
rials. Lacking a guitar and sufficiently chiseled bone structure,
I looked more like Watts, the blond, drum-playing tomboy
(not a lesbian) played by Mary Stuart Masterson in the 1987
teen angst drama *Some Kind of Wonderful*. As a fan of Mary
Stuart Masterson, I will emphasize that this is not in and of
itself a bad thing. But I had just moved to a new town and
just about everyone who met me was meeting me for the first
time and had little else to go on. Moreover, that town was
Los Angeles, a place with major holdings in the business of
exaggerated femininity. If I'd been in a city with a more
unisex fashion sensibility, if I'd been in some flannel-shirted,
polar-fleeced place like Missoula or Portland or Boulder, my
habiliment might have coded entirely differently. But as it
was, my all-wheel-drive sport-utility wagon, Tweety Bird
hair, and makeup arsenal composed of tinted sunscreen and
eight different flavors of Chapstick drew little in the way of

male attention. I did, however, catch women checking me out all the time. Instead of taking this as constructive feedback, I felt flattered and triumphant.

I was flattered in the way a famous or otherwise accomplished person is flattered when he receives an honorary degree from a university that would never have let him in if he'd actually applied. I was flattered because I believed I belonged to a special category of women for whom many of the conventional rules of hotness (long hair, long fingernails, a skilled and thought-out approach to cosmetics) are rendered irrelevant. This is to say I counted myself among the ranks of straight woman who are ever-so-slightly unstraight. I'm not talking about being bisexual. I mean something more like "biologically straight, culturally lesbian." Think of it as another version of the gentile who has no interest in converting to Judaism but nonetheless celebrates most Jewish holidays and occasionally uses Yiddish expressions (as it happens, I am in this category as well). The writer and scholar Terry Castle coined the term "apparitional lesbian," which she described as the ghostlike presence of love between women throughout much of history and literature. In homage to Castle (of whom I am a fan, unsurprisingly), I have dabbled with my own coinage, the "aspirational lesbian," otherwise known as the basically hetero broad for whom the more glamorous expressions of dykery hold a distinct if perpetually enigmatic allure.

Ever the striver, I approach lesbians as though I've been preapproved for their company. I approach them as though I'm their future best friend, the one person at the party they're really going to be glad they met. Walking into a room of strangers, I'll make a beeline for the women with the smart haircuts and "statement" eyewear, and if they seem less than

interested in talking to me I'll be hurt and slightly taken
aback. I am, after all, one of them—or as close as I can get
without actually being *one of them*. My hairdresser of the last
ten years is a lesbian, as was the one for five years before that.
When I feel low I watch YouTube videos of Fran Lebowitz
holding forth on topics like Jane Austen and the irrelevance
of algebra and I feel instantly better. My preferred scent for
soaps and lotions is—you guessed it—lavender. I'm an
honest-to-goodness fan of Willa Cather. As a kid, I worshipped the child movie actress Jodie Foster and the teen
television actress Kristy McNichol. At twenty-nine, I decided to move from New York City to Nebraska in part
because I'd met a couple of middle-aged lesbians who lived
on a farm, and somehow their existence signified a rightness
with the world that I had never encountered elsewhere. At
fifteen, I turned on the television and stumbled on Oprah
Winfrey interviewing members of a lesbian sorority (a revo-
lutionary enterprise at the time) and thought these were the
coolest, most impressive, articulate, and poised women I'd
ever seen. They wore businesslike blazers and spoke in pre-
cise, unapologetic tones that defied everything I'd ever
associated with sororities. They were the kind of women
I wanted to be. Even if I didn't want to be in their beds, I
wanted to be in their club.

Over the years, I believe I've gotten as close to the lesbian inner sanctum as a straight girl can get. Even if I don't
officially belong to the club, I am a de facto member. I am
an honorary dyke. (I am so thoroughly one that I'm allowed
to use the word *dyke* in the transgressive, reappropriative
manner that real lesbians often do.)

Still, the getup of my early thirties pushed the boundar-
ies of de facto. I was not shaving my legs with regularity. I

once, in what I now realize was a cruel, self-serving gesture
that I'd construed as hospitality, asked a stone butch out on a
date. ("Stone butch" being the official term for lesbians on
the most masculine end of the spectrum.) I did not admit
it was a date, of course. The woman was an author visiting
from out of town. I'd recorded a radio interview with her
about her latest book and, after doing so, asked if she knew
anyone in Los Angeles. When she said no, I invited her to
dinner. I told myself I did this out of empathy for the loneliness of being in a strange city with nothing to do. But this
was more than a little disingenuous. I encountered out-of-
towners all the time and almost never worried about their
loneliness. I also knew from firsthand experience that there's
nothing most traveling authors would rather do than order
hotel room service, watch crappy TV for a few hours, and
fall asleep by nine.

The truth was I wanted this woman to like me. More
precisely, I wanted my honors to be recognized. I fetched
her at her hotel in the Subaru and took her to a cozy spot in
Laurel Canyon. We split a bottle of wine and ordered lav-
ishly on her publisher's (also at the time technically my publisher's) dime. About halfway through the meal I got nervous
and let it drop that I was straight. I made reference to an old
boyfriend. Fearing that wasn't enough, I made reference to
the challenges of finding a new boyfriend. She gave me a
look that suggested she could see not only right through me
but also through the insulting fraud of all honorary distinc-
tions everywhere. Shame radiated off my body like a sun-
burn. The author's hotel was in West Hollywood. That is to
say, it was within walking distance of any number of bars
where she could have picked up any number of women who
wouldn't have wasted her time with this pitiful sport fishing.

("Sport fishing," according to the gay lexicon, is when a straight girl flirts with a lesbian but has no intention of following through. This fishing is just for "sport" because no one eats any fish. Get it?)

Not that my gun shyness didn't belie some measure of sincere interest. For as long as I can remember, females held infinitely more fascination than males. Not in a sexual way but in a visceral way, in an *existential* way. This is common, of course, in young girls and even in adult women. Women are more colorful, more layered, more interesting to watch. But as a child I felt a need to study them almost like textbooks. Having no older sister (or younger one, for that matter), I looked to outside peers for clues on how to be female. Just about every year I made a point of picking out some other girl, usually a slightly older girl with whom I'd never exchanged a word, and labeling her "the mystery girl." I would then proceed to observe her in a manner you might call opportunistic stalking. This did not mean approaching her or seeking any direct interaction but, rather, watching her intensely when I happened to spot her in the schoolyard or at the local pool. I would note the make and color of her bicycle, the type of book bag she carried, whether or not she wore socks with her tennis shoes.

The mystery girls were never girly girls. They were almost always quietly tomboyish, or at least marked by a degree of gravitas and self-possession that separated them from the great, giggling masses. There was something to learn from all of them. From Gretchen, my first mystery girl, who was in fourth grade when I was in second, I got the idea of coveting a blue Raleigh three-speed and wearing tennis socks with pompoms on the backs. From Dawn, a delicate-featured flutist I targeted in junior high school, I learned that boat-neck shirts were ideal for showing off prominent collarbones, which I could see were very good things to have. In high school and even college, I kept multiple mystery girls in a steady rotation, though with the bulk of my observational energy now focused on males, I tended to appreciate these girls mostly in fleeting moments. There was the violinist Elizabeth and the beguiling manner in which she lifted her expensive instrument from its case and, as she arranged her music on the stand, held it casually in her left hand as though it were any old thing. There was the track star Julie with her tanned, coltish legs. In college there was Victoria, who mounted futuristic productions of Ibsen plays, wasn't afraid to eat alone in the dining hall, and drove an old Peugeot with plates from a southern state (it was rumored that her mother was a United Daughter of the Confederacy; it was also rumored that Victoria was either bisexual or a lesbian).

Though I had a friendly acquaintanceship with Victoria, the rest of the mystery girls were almost complete mysteries—people I barely knew. They weren't major preoccupations, more like miniature hobbies, objects of passing intrigue that appeared in my line of vision from time to time. It's probably worth mentioning that my mother was an early proponent of the mystery-girl concept. When, as an impressionable seven-year-old, I told her about Gretchen, whose name I didn't even know at the time and who I must have brought up by way of expressing my desire to copy her in some fashion (via pompom socks or a Raleigh bike), my mother said I was too young for a three-speed but that I could instead amuse myself by thinking about "this person you so admire" and trying to learn more about her. I'm inclined to say my mother suggested we find out where Gretchen lived by following her home from the pool (an activity on which my mother would have had to accompany me, since I wasn't allowed to cavort around the neighborhood alone), but that sounds crazy now. It sounds genuinely stalkerish, though some version of stalking was not necessarily out of my mother's character. (She sometimes followed me to school for fear I'd be abducted; she took walks at night so she could see into neighbors' lit windows.)

Yet stalking had no place in the equation. It wasn't that I wanted to get to know these girls. It wasn't that I'd necessarily even have liked them if I had. It was that I wanted to *be* them. Blond, pale-skinned, seemingly comfortable in her own skin, Gretchen was essentially a better version of blond, pale-skinned, hyper-self-conscious me. As with the girls that followed, Gretchen was apt to be spotted alone. She came across to me as a free agent, a doer of her own thing. Never lodged in a bramble of tittering, whispering, terrifying girls, never wearing a uniform of any kind, never with her parents (and now that I think of it, I suspect I unconsciously assumed that Gretchen, like a Peanuts comic strip character, had no parents, that they were irrelevant to her existence), Gretchen was a series of portraits: girl with bicycle, girl with schoolbooks, girl with tanned legs and white pompom socks. Like Elizabeth and Julie and probably even Victoria, she was almost certainly less autonomous than I imagined her to be. Almost certainly she was just as social and cliquish as the girls I had deemed unworthy of mystery. Almost certainly this was true of all my mystery girls. For all I know, Gretchen went to college and joined an old-fashioned sorority and never ate a meal alone for the rest of her life. For all I know, Victoria placed her tray on the conveyor belt after those solitary dinners, reported directly to the nearest keg party, and spent the remainder of the evening doing beer bongs with the lacrosse team—though perhaps not the men's lacrosse team.

With the exception of Victoria, who attracted me just enough to petrify me, it never crossed my mind to do something like sleep with or even kiss one of my mystery girls. This would have ruined the mystery on countless levels, starting with the fact that I'd probably have to have a conversation with them first. But since honorary dykedom almost always requires a trial membership in legitimate dykedom, I knew I'd eventually have to give it the old college try.

College tries, of course, are best suited for college. Ever the late bloomer, I waited a few years until graduate school. Entering the pleasantly dingy, ambition-stoked classrooms of a certain writing program at a certain university on the Upper West Side of Manhattan, I found much of the expected fare: egotistical yet painfully thin-skinned young men obsessed with finding literary agents, socially awkward poets, and women seeming to want only to write about their early sexual experiences. But there was something else, too. There was a grand coterie of lesbians, a posse of women whose hybrid of urban grit and flinty Martha's Vineyard–ishness (black leather jackets with plaid flannel shirts, ragg wool sweaters, Doc Marten boots, and silver jewelry) captivated me so thoroughly that I soon forgot there was anyone else in the program at all. "The whole place is lesbian!" I'd trumpet to friends on the outside. "Every damn one of them!"

There was Debbie, a serious-minded former newspaper reporter. There was Annie, a tiny person who wore enormous Irish wool sweaters and had also worked as a reporter. Her girlfriend was a modern dancer. They were a major power couple as far as I was concerned. There was Lynn, a particularly cute one in my opinion, who wore a tough-looking motorcycle jacket but had a soft, floppy haircut and freckles that reminded me of Melissa Gilbert as Laura Ingalls on the *Little House on the Prairie* television series (I'd been a major fan, natch). There were plenty more in the posse: Karen and Katherine and Jessica and so on. But as a point of fact, they weren't all gay. Their weekend gatherings included plenty of straight girls who, like me, were either unwilling or unable to get with the standard-issue feminine program—in other words, mystery girls demystified. On weekends we'd sit around someone's apartment drinking cheap Merlot and listening to the gynocentric musical stylings of newcomers like Joan Osborne and Jewel.

I never felt anything but totally at ease at these parties. I felt both appreciated and not particularly singled out, as if my presence were a bottle of average-tasting wine that would be unremarked upon but happily consumed nonetheless. One Saturday night, however, I arrived at the party and was met with looks that suggested amusement, concern, and vindication all at once.

"So what's up? How are you?" they all basically said in unison.

I replied that I was fine. A little stressed with schoolwork, but whatever.

"You doing okay with all of this?" asked Annie.

"All of what?" I asked.

I have historically prided myself on my powers of perception. Yet I'd apparently missed a whole series of signals emitted by a certain classmate, another lesbian who was only tangentially in our gang and whose real name happened to be the same as Lynn's real name (I will call her Lynn B.).

Earlier that week, Lynn B. had invited me on an outing,

to a swim meet, specifically. She did not know any of the swimmers personally, she said, but was enough of a sports enthusiast to regard her recent enrollment in the university as an occasion to cheer on the Lady Lions as they hurled themselves through the tangy waters of the campus pool. Seeing the invitation as nothing more than a gesture of friendship, I'd accepted, though no set arrangements were made.

But evidently the gesture was more than friendly. Arriving at the Saturday night meet-up, I was shocked to find myself at the center of a major piece of gossip.

"We hear you and Lynn B. might be an item," Debbie said, sounding like a worried mother but also a bit excited.

"What?" I yelped. "What are you talking about?

I was then informed that this was no innocent swim meet but a perilously spring-loaded tête-à-tête ("She asked you to a *sporting event*?" Annie bellowed. "Get a *clue!*") and that going through with it was essentially tantamount to letting a man buy you dinner and then going back to his apartment to "borrow a book." I would, in other words, be sending strong signals, if not downright asking for it.

"Don't worry," Annie said. "I'll take care of it."

From there, the gathering resumed its standard rhythms. Drinks were poured, smokes were lit, the door buzzer heralded a stream of friends and friends of friends and Indian food delivery. We talked about our writing projects and about how this new artist Jewel probably wouldn't go anywhere. (So intense was my connoisseurship of girl singer–songwriters that within days of Jewel's debut release I'd not only purchased and listened to the CD, I already hated it.)

Lynn and I ended up leaving the party at the same time that night. Emerging from the steamy clutches of the overheated building and tiptoeing across the black ice and blown trash of upper Broadway, we returned to the subject of my would-be date. I said something about being an unintentional tease, about feeling bad about it, about feeling somewhat unmoored in my life lately and like someone had clipped off the ends of my antennae. I was missing signs, dialing things out. She told me not to sweat it too much. Then she gave me a nervous glance and said, "If you're going to sleep with any of us, just promise it'll be me."

Life, of course, is a process of elimination. To grow up and get to know yourself is primarily an exercise in taking things off the table. It's not that I didn't want to sleep with Lynn. I did—at least I didn't *not* want to. But as our initial romp (terrifying, fascinating, somewhat performative on my part) faded into a string of more lackluster encounters, I found myself in a sped-up version of many of my previous, long-term relationships, my desire waning in predictable increments in just a few months' time. First I was happy to skip the main stage activities. Then I just wanted to cuddle. Then I just wanted to sit on the couch and watch TV.

What was clear almost immediately about this little adventure was that I was in it less for the sex than for the sociology. The thing I really loved to do with Lynn was talk to her— about lots of subjects, but about lesbian stuff in particular. I wanted to break down the different levels of femmeness and butchery: femme, high femme, stone femme, soft butch, stone butch, sport dyke, and so on. I wanted to discuss the fact that Jodie Foster and Kristy McNichol both grew up to be big-time "members of the church." On a couple of occasions, Lynn took me on field trips to lesbian bars, one of which was tucked away improbably on the ground floor of some generic midtown office building. It was not a place for dabblers. Its clientele covered a cultural and socioeconomic spectrum I had never before seen in one room. There were working-class butches with unironic mullets, femmes who looked like mafia wives, and full-bore trannies. The whole scene freaked me out enough to make me realize that I was not a lesbian so much as someone who appreciated a good haircut. And contrary to my preconceptions, these could in no way be counted upon as a standard feature of the gay female population.

Lynn humored me for a while, allowing our relationship to remain inside my comfort zone of mix-tape exchanges and mostly platonic sleepovers bathed in the glow of scented candles that, by two a.m., had burned themselves into lavender puddles on the top of her bookshelf. In the end, though, I just didn't have it in me to play for the other team. I was twenty-five. There was a lot in the world I was still trying on for size. Lynn was thirty-four and had never had sex with a man. She was the real deal, a "gold star lesbian." For my birthday, she gave me a jewelry box made of beveled glass and silver. It was exquisite, at once delicate and sturdy. I loved it. I knew I had to end things.

Lynn wasn't surprised but she cried anyway. This irritated me. It also gave me a new appreciation for men, who are expected to deal with emotional women in much the same way they're expected to help lift heavy objects. They have to sit there with the blubbering and pretend it isn't making them horribly uncomfortable. They have to try to not let on that they're doing a furious calculation in their heads as to how long they have to stay before they can walk away without looking like an asshole.

But Lynn's emotionalism pulled the veil off something else, too. It revealed something thorny and discomfiting,

something that felt at once flattering and insulting, something that I'd probably known subconsciously throughout
our entire affair but swatted away whenever it crept into my
awareness. And that was that even though Lynn was the senior executive in the relationship and I was the intern, even
though she was the veteran dyke and I was the honorary dyke,
even though she wore a full-fledged classic black leather
biker jacket and I wore a vintage suede coat and miniskirts
with tights and chunky Italian loafers, she was playing the
girl part and I was playing the guy part. She was the crier
and I was the instigator of the tears. She was leaving phone
messages and I was taking a little too long to call back. She
was the clinger and I was the puller away. She was the femme
and I was the butch. I didn't like it one bit.

   Among the men I dated over the next several years were
an airline pilot and a guy who chopped his own wood.

Almost two decades later, I now know that it wasn't Lynn
who was making me the butch. I was one already. I had
always been one. And even today, when I have long hair
and a husband and have resigned myself to dusting on a little
makeup if I'm going somewhere fancy, I'm still a butch. I'm
a particular kind of butch you find in straight women, a
butch not defined by clothes or hair or physicality but by
something more essential, something perhaps identifiable
only to other butches of this genre. You could call us secret
butches but that wouldn't be quite right, since whatever it is
that makes us this way is the dominant chord of our character. Indeed, this butchness hides in plain sight. It's more like
a shadow, an aura, a *phantom*. It's not that we don't want to
play traditional women's roles. It's not that we don't want

to take care of our families or have beautiful, meticulously kept homes or that we can't have strong opinions about furniture upholstery or cake decoration or attachment parenting. It's that we're going to express these opinions and carry out these practices with a certain anti-girliness, a certain lack of bullshit. We do not, for instance, elevate our vocal pitch at the end of declarative sentences as though asking a question. We do not apply makeup in public. We do not wear enormous diamond rings to yoga class with the intention of sticking them in our neighbor's face while holding the Warrior II position. Being a phantom butch should not be confused with being a tomboy. Tomboyhood is a childlike state. Butch, phantom or otherwise, is an adult-woman state. The tomboy may be the precursor to the butch but sometimes it's just the precursor to being good at sports, which leads to popularity in school and is just as likely to result in getting elected homecoming queen as getting mistaken for Martina Navratilova.

Some women who seem to aspire to phantom butchery don't actually have the goods. Meanwhile, some who you'd never consciously think of in such terms are bathing in it. Madonna, for instance, has always been too invested in her fuckability to be a butch, though Beyoncé most certainly qualifies. Many actual lesbians don't even make the cut. Portia de Rossi, partner of Ellen DeGeneres, is not a phantom butch. However, Ellen's former partner Anne Heche, who is now married to a man and therefore a "hasbian," most definitely is.

Patti Smith, the indisputable queen mother of honorary dykedom, and her protégée Chrissie Hynde are both so butch that phantom doesn't even enter into the equation (ditto Sonic Youth's Kim Gordon, even more so postdivorce). Sarah McLaughlin may be the face of the Lilith Fair and a de facto honorary dyke, but she's no butch. Her vibe is too much like the Anthropologie* store, floral and curlicue and bursting with too many ambient layers (necklaces atop necklaces, fur-lined collars, bejeweled bustiers worn with jeans; a look, admittedly, that I aspired to incorporate into my toe-ring-and-Subaru look before accepting that I just didn't have the energy for it).

All of this is arguable, of course[†]. You are no doubt at this moment silently quibbling with me over several of these examples. Either that or I lost you at "butch"—at least the idea of my being one. Again, please understand I'm not a butch in the conventional sense. I have long hair on which I spend too much money maintaining the blondness of my youth. I get manicures and pedicures like every other chick in the industrialized world, or at least I have since roughly 2001, when it suddenly became illegal to leave your house without painted toenails. As casual as my wedding was, I wore a real wedding gown with a veil. That veil turned out to be the single most delightful thing I have ever placed on my head and perhaps my entire body. I felt like if I began to skip down the sidewalk,

---

*Despite the special relationship between honorary dykes and shabby-chic door hardware (a relationship based on the fetishization of female-only households, since there is not a man, gay or straight, currently alive who would, of his own volition, replace a perfectly functional doorknob with one made of blue "magma glass"), Anthropologie is not butch, phantom or otherwise. It is Disney with a slightly more sophisticated but no less carefully engineered aesthetic. It is to adult women what princesses are to little girls. It is a twirling motion in the form of an international brand.

[†]What *is* undeniably butch is Cost Plus World Market. Specializing in exotic and ethnographically diverse housewares for budget-minded battleaxes of all ages (plus robust wine selections and stunning assortments of British crackers), its stores are emporiums of phantom butchosity, a paean to the world-traveling, solo dinner-party-throwing imaginings of women who believe themselves to have advanced beyond the Pier One Imports stage but remain too invested in their perceived bohemianism to shop at Restoration Hardware. The place mat selection alone has, at times, left me breathless.

the veil would form a sail and lift me into the air. I remember climbing into a taxi on my wedding night and thinking that I never wanted to take it off. I remember thinking, *In less than twenty minutes I'm going to have to take this off and never wear it again.* I remember—and will never stop remembering—the pangs of grief that accompanied this realization. In that moment, I was just like any other bride in the world. I was a little girl who didn't want to take off her princess costume. I was, if only for a few fleeting moments, a willing and even ecstatic participant in womanhood's most sentimental mien.

Still, when I try to make sense of my honorary dykedom, especially as it manifests in my life at the moment, I can't help but think it's at least in part a reaction to the gaudy, petty horrors now endemic to what we've come to call "women's culture." By this I mean all the crap in the media that suggests that not only are women a special interest group, they're a group whose primary interest is themselves. I mean the fetishistic attention paid to makeovers and diets and weddings and baby showers and enormous walk-in closets as proof of a husband's love for his wife. I mean moms who are obsessed with their motherhood and single women who are obsessed with their singleness. I mean most romantic comedies and most novels with stiletto heels or martini glasses on the covers and every yogurt commercial ever made. I mean the girls' toy aisles in stores that are an ocean of pink: pink Scrabble games, pink guitars, and pink guns. I mean the hair and eyelash extensions that have become commonplace. I mean the fact that there is nothing unusual about seeing businesswomen walking down the street in six-inch heels. Gone are the 1980s, when women tucked their pumps into their briefcases and commuted to work in power suits and running shoes. Gone are the 1970s, with their conspicuous body hair and unapologetic strands of gray pulled into unkempt buns held up with leather stick barrettes. Here in the era of bosomy, spray-tanned, baby-crazed bling, femininity has become a cartoon version of itself. It is at once exaggerated in its presentation and reductive in its implications. It's enough to make a butch out of anyone who just wants a comfortable pair of shoes.

Maybe this cartoonish femininity is the reason so many women's clothing stores are such hideous funhouses. It's certainly the reason that nearly all of my apparel purchasing is done on the computer. While it's true that online shopping incurs all sorts of shipping costs and means constantly having to return things, I am not exaggerating when I say I would rather stand in line at the post office for forty-five minutes than at Banana Republic for fifteen seconds. Walking into a women's clothing store makes me feel like I'm walking into a slumber party attended by my least favorite girls in the class (or in the case of Ann Taylor or Talbots, the mothers of those girls). But catalog shopping, online or in print, is quiet and personal. It's inherently literary. It's about designating ordinary-looking sweaters and jackets as "yachtwear." It's about never using color names like yellow and green when there's gamboge and malachite. And in the case of my favorite catalog, the Title Nine women's sports apparel catalog, it's about giving honorary dykedom an official handbook.

Named for the history-making federal law allowing women equal access to sports in schools, the Title Nine company has a feminist bent and a prep-school-meets-Phish-concert aesthetic. Its models aren't typical models but, rather, "real women" whose bodies are muscular rather than skeletal and whose faces, though endowed with well-above-average bone structure, are also endowed with the kinds of slightly crooked smiles and traces of crow's-feet that would normally be Photoshopped into oblivion. They have strong shoulders and ripped abs and, best of all, brief biographical profiles perversely presented in the vein of Playboy playmate squibs. "Steph is a professional climber, base jumper and author." How does she unwind? She "likes to clean things." (Things on the order of antique auto parts, mind you; not kitchen floors.) Niko, pictured hula hooping in a flowered halter dress, is a mom whose special skills include "uphill battles." Yhazi is a "business owner" who drives an '84 Volkswagen bus and is an avid practitioner of the Brazilian martial art/dance/music hybrid capoeira.

As they model the fleece jackets, skorts, sports bras, and dresses that come with names like Tomboy Wrap dress, Dauntless dress, and Excellence dress, the phantom-dyke-centered narratives play out in charmingly allegorical fashion. There's Allison (semipro cyclist and obsessive knitter) throwing her head back in laughter as she gathers wood with Katie (lawyer and kiteboarder), who sports pigtails and *carries a chainsaw.* A few pages later in the catalog, we see Lucy bundled up in wool leggings and a chunky sweater coat knocking on a cabin door. She carries a tasteful ceramic dish and a bottle of wine. Snow covers the ground, a holiday wreath hangs from the door. You can almost smell the chimney smoke. Could this be the home of Katie? Could that smoke be the vapor of her hard-earned firewood? Could Allison live there, too? Maybe Steph and Niko are in the kitchen, stirring up hot toddies and comparing notes about their uphill battles.

Of course they are! Better yet, it's a potluck! Lucy has

brought her famous homemade lasagna. We are someplace like the Berkshire Mountains in western Massachusetts. We are travelers across a wintry landscape dusted with fir trees and Subarus and dykes of the honorary and nonhonorary varieties alike (not to mention home of Kim Gordon, Smith College, and the farmhouse of Rachel Maddow and her partner of many years). We are caught in the cozy, sporty, always slightly sweaty embrace of Title Nine, a world where a fancy evening out means wearing your favorite Intrepid Hoodie dress with tights and a pair of Frye boots, a world where skinny jeans are forever supplanted by cargo pants, a world where, if Paris Hilton were standing on the corner of Main and King Streets in Northampton, you'd think a spaceship had landed nearby and off-loaded one of its more disposable life-forms. If such a starlet appeared in Title Nine's pages, she would be incorporated into a two-page spread depicting a mountain rescue of dilettante Mount Everest climbers buried in an avalanche. She would be thrown over the shoulder of Katie, who carries an ice axe in one hand and a coffee thermos in the other as she ferries Paris out of harm's way. Wearing the snowstopper pant with microfleece inner face ($119), Katie installs the poor nymph in her cabin, where she lays her by the fire and nurses her back to health on vegan stew, though not before flinging a Jeanette Winterson book at her and telling her not to come back until she's manned up enough to qualify as a woman.

I love the Title Nine catalog because it reminds me of the girl posse from my graduate school days. I love it because it reminds me of Gretchen and Dawn and Jodie Foster and Kristy McNichol and those sorority sisters on *Oprah*. It takes me back to my fascination with Victoria and my affection for Lynn and my eternal fondness for the Nebraska farm women. It makes me forgive myself a little for my sport fishing venture with the author who knew no one in town. And even though it traffics in its own special brand of sentimentalized womanhood, even though it's engaged in that tyrannical "women can do it all!" messaging that makes female CEOs feel bad about themselves if they're not also kiteboarders and mothers of three, it reminds me what the black lesbian poet Audre Lorde (who I know about courtesy of Lynn's candle-wax-ravaged bookcase) said about the essence of feminism: "The true feminist deals out of a lesbian consciousness whether or not she ever sleeps with women."

Put another way: You don't have to take communion to be a member of the church.

There's more than one way to be a person. Actually, there are more than two or three ways. You'd think that was obvious, but I find that often it is not. The world is essentially a collection of teams. Life is a process of deciding which ones we're going to join. As a person who never liked teams, it makes sense that the one with which I'd feel the most camaraderie would be the one I could never authentically join. Still, like a die-hard sports fan, my devotion defines me. I will always, no matter how crowded the room, find the lesbians the way a golden retriever finds a tennis ball. I will always be *this close* to cutting my hair short again. I will be very sad if I never get to meet Fran Lebowitz. I still have the jewelry box Lynn gave me. I don't have expensive jewelry, but this box, now slightly chipped and tarnished, is where I keep the pieces I like best. It holds gifts from my husband and maybe even from an old boyfriend or two. It holds some birthday presents from close friends. It holds a couple of pairs of my mother's earrings and even more earrings that I bought my-self. It holds the things that, when I put them on, don't make me think, *This is fancy* or even, *This is beautiful* but, rather, *This is me.* It's all so predictable. It's all so transparent, such a cliché. It's all such an honor.

DIFFERENCE MAKER

The first child whose life I tried to make a difference in was Maricela. She was twelve years old and in the sixth grade at a middle school in the San Gabriel Valley, about a half hour's drive from my house near downtown Los Angeles. We'd been matched by the Big Brothers Big Sisters program. It had taken a while to get my assignment, as there were far more women volunteers than men and there often weren't enough girls to go around. But when the volunteer coordinator finally called, he told me I'd be great for Maricela and that she was well worth the wait. Though I'd wanted to be in the "community-based program," where kids went on excursions with volunteers and were allowed to visit their homes, there wasn't sufficient need so I was put in the "school-based program." This meant Maricela would be excused from class twice a month to meet with me in an empty classroom.

On our first visit I brought art supplies—glue and glitter and stencils you could use to draw different types of horses. I hadn't been told much about her, only that she had a lot of younger siblings and often got lost in the shuffle at home. Her family's apartment was close enough to the school that she could walk. She explained to me that her route took her past an ice cream truck every day but that she never had money to buy anything from it. She suggested we go to the ice cream truck together but I explained we weren't supposed to leave the school grounds. In fact, we were supposed to stay in the classroom. The classrooms were arranged around a courtyard, as is typical of California elementary and middle schools. Maricela spent most of our first meeting skulking around in the doorway, calling out to friends who were playing kickball in the courtyard. I sat at a desk tracing glittery horses, telling myself she'd come to me when she was ready.

The second child I tried to make a difference with was Nikki. I met her when I was transferred from the school-based program into the community-based program after it was determined that Maricela was merely using me to get out of class and therefore needed "different kinds of supports." Nikki was fifteen. She lived with her mother, brother, grandmother, and an indeterminate number of other relatives in a crowded apartment in South L.A. Her mother worked as a home health care aide. Another brother had left the household before he turned eighteen, though she didn't go into much detail. Nikki had requested a Big Sister of her own volition, writing on her application that she needed "guidance in life." We met for the first time in an office at Big Brothers Big Sisters' Los Angeles headquarters. Her mother brought her to the meeting and they both sat quietly while an employee facilitated a rather halting conversation about what kinds of things Nikki liked to do and what particular strengths I might have as a mentor.

I can't remember exactly what I said, but I'm sure it was

something about being available to help her with home-work, especially English assignments. Though I would end up being Nikki's Big Sister for more than three years, I never once helped her with homework. I did take her to an ex-perimental theater production of *Tosca* that my neighbor had directed and which Nikki, to her enormous credit, sat through without complaint. But mostly she wanted to go to the mall. These were outings on which she examined hand-bags at the Hello Kitty store while I feigned enthusiasm and scraped the reaches of my mind for conversation topics that might lead to some form of bonding or a teachable moment. With the exception of one occasion when I tried to explain that President Bush most likely did not, as she put it (actually as Kanye West had suggested on live television), "hate black people" but, rather, had policies that were unfavorable to-ward all but the wealthiest Americans, such moments never arose. When she came over to my house, she spent much of the time on my computer sending instant messages to friends and taking self-portraits (the term "selfies" had not yet been coined) with the Photo Booth application. A few times I ducked into the frame and the computer snapped the two of us together making silly faces. This was such an inaccurate representation of our actual rapport that I was embarrassed. It was as if we were imitating a Big and Little Sister. Or at least one of us was.

Later I found out Nikki actually had several different mentors from several different volunteer organizations. They came with different areas of expertise: help with college ap-plications and financial aid, help finding a summer job, help with "girl empowerment," whatever that meant. This partly explained why nearly every time I asked her if she'd been to a particular place—to the science center or the art museum or the Staples Center to see an L.A. Sparks women's basketball game—she told me, yes, some other mentor had taken her.

I was thirty-five years old when I worked with Maricela and thirty-six when I met Nikki. These were years I would later come to see as the beginning of the second act of my adult life. If the first act, which is to say college through age thirty-two, had been mostly taken up by delirious career ambition and almost compulsive moving between houses and apartments and regions of the country, the second act seemed mostly to be about appreciating the value of staying put. I'd bought a house that I wasn't planning on moving out of anytime soon. I was in a city that was feeling more and more like home. And though I could well imagine being talked out of my single life and getting married if the right person and circumstances came along, one thing that seemed increasingly unlikely to budge was my lack of desire to have children. After more than a decade of being told that I'd wake up one morning at age thirty or thirty-three or, God forbid, forty, to the ear-splitting peals of my biological clock, I'd failed to capitulate in any significant way. I would still look at a woman pushing a baby stroller and feel more pity than envy. In fact, I felt no envy at all, only relief that I wasn't her. It was like looking at someone with an amputated limb or terrible scar. I almost had to look away.

I recognized that my reaction was extreme. I was also willing to concede that I was possibly in denial. All the things people say to people like me were things I'd said to myself countless times. If I met the right partner, maybe I'd want a child because I'd want it *with him*. If I went to therapy to deal with whatever neuroses could plausibly be blamed on my own childhood, maybe I'd get over myself and trust in my ability not to repeat its more negative aspects. If I only understood that you don't have to like other children in order to be hopelessly smitten with and devoted to your own (as it happens, this was my parents' stock phrase: "We don't like other children, we just like you"), I would stop taking my aversion to kids kicking airplane seats and shrieking in restaurants as a sign that I should never, ever have any myself. After all, it's such a tiny percentage of women—5 or 6 percent, according to the tiny handful of entities studying such things—that genuinely feel that motherhood isn't for them. This is the most minor of minorities. Was I really that exceptional? And if I was, why did I have names picked out for the children I didn't want?

For all of this I had reasons. I had reasons springing forth from reasons. They ran the gamut from "don't want to be pregnant" to "don't want to make someone deal with me when I'm dying." (And, for the record, I've never met a woman of any age and any level of inclination to have children who doesn't have names picked out.) Chief among them, though, was my belief that I'd be a bad mother. Not in the Joan Crawford mode but in the mode of parents you sometimes see who obviously love their kids but pretty clearly do not love their own lives. For every way I could imagine being a good mother, for all the upper-middle-class embellishments I'd offer in the form of artful children's books and educational toys and decent schools—magnet, private, or otherwise—I could imagine ten ways that I'd botch the job irredeemably.

More than that, though, I simply felt no calling to be a parent. As a role, as *my* role, it felt inauthentic and inorganic. It felt unnecessary. It felt like not what I was supposed to be doing with my life. What I was supposed to be doing was writing and reading and teaching and giving talks at colleges.

What I was supposed to be was a mentor, not a mom. My contribution to society was all about not contributing more people to it but, rather, doing something (and I felt this in a genuine way, not in an aphoristic or guilt-ridden one) for the ones that were already here. Ones like Maricela and Nikki.

Except Maricela and Nikki didn't really need me all that much. Or at least they didn't need *me* specifically. They each might have benefited from a real big sister, someone who shared their DNA and/or at least a common interest or two. But there wasn't anything about my particular skill set that was likely to improve their quality of life in any measurable way. After Nikki graduated from high school and aged out of Big Brothers Big Sisters (and went to college, I should add), I took a break from kid-related do-gooderism for a few years. During that time, I married my boyfriend, a man who seemed only slightly more interested in potential parenthood than I was, which is to say not enough to explore the issue in any depth. When I decided to return to volunteerism, I was determined to up the ante. So I became a court-appointed advocate for children in the foster care system.

Court-appointed advocacy is a national program designed to facilitate communication in foster care cases that are too complicated for any one social worker or lawyer or judge (all crushingly overworked) to keep track of. The advocate's job is to fit together the often disparate pieces of information about a child's situation and create a coherent narrative for the judge. This narrative takes the form of written reports submitted to the court several times a year and is supplemented with actual appearances in court, where the advocate can address the judge directly. Sometimes the information is simple: *This child wants to play baseball but needs transportation to the practices and the games.* Sometimes it's gothic:

This child is being locked in the basement by her foster mother because she's become violent and the state insurance plan won't cover her antipsychotic medication. Advocates are required to see the children at least once a month, and are encouraged to take them places and help them with schoolwork. But they are not mentors as much as investigators—sometimes even de facto judges, since judges often rely heavily on advocates' recommendations when making their rulings.

Like my interest in being a Big Sister, the urge to be a child advocate was mostly an urge to inject something into my life that, for lack of a better way of putting it, had nothing to do with my life. As huge in many ways as that life was, it often gave the sensation of an isometric exercise requiring the foot to repeatedly draw very small, perfect circles in the air. I wanted some bigger, messier circles. Moreover, I didn't want these circles to intersect with anything related to my professional career. If I'd wanted to find volunteer opportunities that kept me in the orbit of my regular crowd, I could have taught creative writing to prisoners or joined the hipsters who worked at drop-in tutoring centers in gentrifying neighborhoods. But I didn't want to go that route. I wanted to be in a different neighborhood entirely.

Children who wind up in foster care aren't just in a different neighborhood. They inhabit a world so dark it may as well exist outside our solar system. This was certainly the case with Matthew, the boy I was assigned to shortly after I completed my advocacy training. Compared with him, Maricela and Nikki might as well have been upper-middle-class children of suburbia, complete with riding lessons and college funds.

Matthew was the child of no one. Of course, that's not literally true. He had parents. At least, he'd had them at one time. But they were permanently out of the picture, as were any number of others who'd endeavored at times to take their place. Matthew was a longtime foster child. He lived in a group home, one of a hundred or so children who had proven incapable of functioning in traditional family settings. He ate his meals when he was told to, watched whatever happened to be on the television in the common room at any given time, and put himself to bed every night. When I met him he was about to turn twelve. He had been living this way on and off since the age of six.

There is very little I am permitted to reveal about Matthew, starting with his name, which is not Matthew (just as Maricela's is not Maricela and Nikki's is not Nikki). I cannot tell you about his parents or what they did to land their son in the child welfare system, but I can tell you that it's about as horrific as anything you can imagine. As with just about everyone else in this story, I cannot provide a physical description of Matthew, but for the sake of giving you something to hold on to I'm going to say he's African American, knobby-kneed, and slightly nearsighted. He's not necessarily any or all of those things but I'm going to plant that image in your mind and move on.

Was Matthew a cute kid? A charming kid? A kid with potential? People seemed to think so when they first met him, but then things had a way of going south. That was the pattern, anyway. His housing history covered the demographic spectrum. I can't give specifics, but let's say there'd been middle-class suburban couples, single moms, gay dads, and large evangelical Christian families. Some had wanted to adopt him but then changed their minds when he started feeling safe enough to test their loyalty by making their lives hell.

On my first meeting with Matthew, he wanted me to do what many advocates do for their assignees and take him to McDonald's for a Happy Meal (the meal of choice, it turns out, for the unhappiest kids in the world). But I wasn't allowed to take him off the grounds of the group home, so we sat in the dining hall and hobbled through a conversation about what my role as his advocate amounted to (he already knew; he'd had one before) and what I might do to help make his life a little better. In my training sessions, I'd learned that it was a good idea to bring a game or toy to break the ice. After much deliberation, I had settled on a pack of cards that asked hundreds of different "would you rather" questions: "Would you rather be invisible or able to read minds?" and "Would you rather be able to stop time or fly?" Matthew's enthusiasm for this activity was middling at best, and when I got to questions like "Would you rather go to an amusement park or a family reunion?" or "Would you rather be scolded by your teacher or by your parents?" I shivered at the stupidity of not having vetted them ahead of time. He had no parents to scold him or family reunions to attend. This was like asking someone with no legs if he'd rather walk or take the bus.

"We don't have to play with these," I said.

"Uh-huh," Matthew said. This would soon be revealed as his standard response to just about everything. It was delivered in the same tone regardless of the context, a tone of impatience mixed with indifference, the tone people use when they're waiting for the other person to stop talking.

The next time I saw him, I was allowed to take him out. I suggested we go to the zoo or to the automotive museum, which had an interactive children's exhibit devoted to the inner workings of cars, but he said he wanted to go shopping at Target. He'd recently had a birthday and received gift cards he wanted to redeem. I would figure out soon enough that currency for most foster kids took the form of gift cards from places like Target or Walmart. The retailers allocated a certain amount for needy children, which meant that social workers and advocates would unceremoniously bestow them on their charges on holidays and birthdays. Matthew's moods, it often seemed, rose and fell with the cards' balances.

On this shopping trip, the first of many, he seemed upbeat, counting and recounting the cash in his pocket (he received a small weekly allowance from the group home) and adding it to the sum total of his gift cards, including a card worth $25 that I'd picked up at the advocacy office and just given him. But, as with so many outings with Matthew, he had enough money to burn a hole in his pocket but not enough to get anything he actually wanted. He wanted something digital, preferably an MP3 player. The only thing in his price range was a Kindle reading device. I tried to explain the concept of saving up a little while longer, but he was determined to buy something right then and there and insisted that he wanted the Kindle. Even after I warned him that he was going to regret the purchase as soon as he got home, that he'd told me he didn't like to read and, besides, he would still have to pay for things to *put on* the Kindle, he remained adamant and took it to the checkout counter, where somehow it turned out he was $25 short anyway. The cashier explained that there were taxes. Also, somehow it appeared that one of his gift cards had already been partially used. Matthew's face began turning red. I couldn't tell if he was going to cry or fly into a rage. There was a line of people behind us.

So I lent him the $25. I lent it on the condition that he'd pay me back in installments.

"Do you know what installments are?" I asked.

"No."

"It's when you give or pay something back in small increments."

I knew he didn't know what *increments* meant, but I couldn't think of an alternative word.

"So now you haven't just gone shopping, you've learned something, too!" I said.

I tried to sound light and jokey. I tried to sound like the opposite of how my mother would have sounded in such a situation. My mother would have pulled me aside and explained the conditions of the agreement in the most serious tones possible. My mother had been a very serious person. She would let you know your shirt was on backward using a voice most people keep in reserve for statements like "Grandpa's had a stroke." At some point in my early forties I realized that my primary goal in just about any verbal exchange is to lighten the mood. If a situation starts to feel too heavy, I will not hesitate to make a joke or say something sarcastic just to push away the feeling of my mother sitting me down and somberly telling me that black and navy don't go together. I do this to a fault. I do it especially with kids and I would do it with Matthew more times than I could count.

Once we were back in the car I found a piece of paper, tore it in half, and wrote out two copies of an IOU, which we both signed. Matthew seemed pleased by this and ran his index finger along the perimeter of the Kindle box as though he'd finally got his hands on a long-coveted item. I gave him command of the radio, and even as he flipped annoyingly between two awful pop stations I found myself basking in the ecstatic glow of altruism. I was a difference maker and a wish fulfiller. When I dropped him off at the group home, the promissory note tucked in his Target shopping bag along with the Kindle and the greasy cardboard plate that held the giant pretzel I'd also bought him, I felt useful. I felt proud. These were not feelings that rolled around all that often in my regular life.

It had been a long time between accomplishments. At least it had become hard to identify them, as most of my goals for any given day or week took the form of tasks, mundane and otherwise, to be dreaded and then either crossed off a list or postponed indefinitely (*finish column, get shirts from dry cleaner, start writing new book*). Rarely did anything seem to warrant any special pride. And though I wanted to believe that I was just bored, the truth lay elsewhere. The truth was that the decision not to have children, which I'd made somewhat unilaterally around the time I signed up to be an advocate, was wrecking me day by day.

As much as I'd never wanted to be a mother, my relationship with my husband had turned me into a bit of a waffler. If I was going to have children with anyone, it was going to be him. He was patient and funny, not to mention tall and handsome and smart. In other words, outstanding dad material. So outstanding, in fact, that wasting such material seemed like an unpardonable crime. Besides, among my personal theories is the idea that it is not possible to fall in love with someone without picturing—whether for one second or one hour or fifty years—what it might be like to combine your genetic goods. It's almost an aspect of courtship, this vision of what your nose might look like smashed up against your loved one's eyes, this imaginary Cubist rendering of the things you hate most about yourself offset by the things you adore most in the other person. And about a year earlier, this small curiosity, combined with the dumb luck of finding and purchasing an elegant, underpriced, much-too-large-for-us house in a foreclosure sale, had proved sufficient cause for switching to the leave-it-to-fate method of birth control. Soon enough, I'd found myself pregnant.

It was as if the house itself had impregnated me, as if it

said, *I have three bedrooms and there are only two of you; what's wrong with this picture?* For eight weeks, I hung in a nervous limbo, thinking my life was either about to become unfathomably enriched or permanently ruined. Then I had a miscarriage. Given that I was forty-one, it was not exactly unexpected. And though there had been nothing enriching about my brief pregnancy, which continued to harass my hormones well after vacating the premises, I was left with something that in a certain way felt worse than permanent ruin. I was left with permanent ambivalence.

My husband was happy about the pregnancy and sad about the miscarriage. I was less sad about the miscarriage, though I undertook to convince myself otherwise by trying to get pregnant again (at least the kind of trying that comes before medically assisted trying, which for a forty-one-year-old may be tantamount to not trying). After three months of dizzying cognitive dissonance (This is *me*, using fertility-test sticks? This is *me*, seeing an acupuncturist?), I walked into the guest room that my husband also used as an office and allowed myself to say the thing I'd been thinking my whole life: I didn't want a baby. I'd never wanted a baby. I'd thought I could talk myself into it, but those talks had failed.

I remember that as we talked I was lying on the cheap platform bed we'd bought in anticipation of a steady flow of out-of-town company. I remember looking at the ceiling and admiring the lines of the window frame and the ceiling molding. I remember that the curtains, which were partly raw silk and looked expensive despite my having bought them for cheap on the JCPenney website, were lifting gently in the breeze. There was bougainvillea outside, along with bees and hummingbirds and mourning doves. There was a big

grassy lawn where the dog rolled around blissfully scratching his back, and a big table on the deck where friends sat
nearly every weekend eating grilled salmon and drinking
wine and complaining about things they knew were a privi-
lege to complain about (the cost of cable television, the noise
of leaf blowers, the problem of not having enough time to
pursue one's art). And as I lay on that bed it occurred to me,
terrifyingly, that all of it might not be enough. It was possible
that such pleasures, while pleasurable enough, were merely
trimmings on a nonexistent tree. It was possible that nothing, not a baby or lack of a baby, not a beautiful house, not
rewarding work, was ever going to make us anything other
than the chronically dissatisfied, perpetual second-guessers
we already were.

"I'm sorry," I said. I meant this a million times over. To
this day, there is nothing I've ever been sorrier about than
my inability to make my husband a father.

"It's okay," he said.

Except it wasn't, really. From there, a third party was
introduced into our marriage. It was not a corporal party
but an amorphous one, a ghoulish presence that functioned
as both cause and effect of the presence that would have
been our child. It had even, in the back of my mind, come to
have a name. It was the Central Sadness; that was the only
thing to call it. It collected around our marriage like soft,
stinky moss. It rooted our arguments and dampened our good
times. It taunted us from the sidelines of our social life (always the barbecues with toddlers underfoot; always a friend's
child interrupting conversations mid-sentence; always the
clubby comparing of notes about Ritalin and dance lessons
and college tuition, which prompted us to feign great interest lest we come across like overgrown children ourselves). It

haunted our sex life. Not since I was a (virginal) teenager had I been so afraid of getting pregnant. I wondered then, as I had a hundred times before when this subject arose, if our marriage was on life support, if at any moment one of us was going to realize that the humane thing to do would be to call it even and then call it a day. How hard, after all, would it be to go back to being the people we'd been before? How easy would it be to stop trying to become the people we apparently didn't have it in ourselves to be?

Compared with this existential torment, foster care advocacy was a cakewalk. Though it was certainly more demanding than Big Brothers Big Sisters, I found it considerably easier—or at least more straightforward—than traditional mentoring. For one thing, advocating for foster kids mostly required dealing with adults. It meant talking to lawyers and meeting with school administrators and sitting around the courthouse all day when there was a hearing. It meant spending a lot of time on the phone with another, much more seasoned advocate, who was supervising me. As onerous as all of this might have been for most people, I found that I loved it. I loved talking to my supervisor. I loved hanging out in the tiny attorneys' lounge outside the courtroom, where there was always a plate of stale supermarket pastries next to the coffeemaker and the lawyers stood around in clusters complaining about the judge, their clients, the whole hopeless gestalt. I was fascinated and moved by the family dramas playing out in the courthouse waiting areas. There, teenage mothers wept into their cell phones and men with shaved heads and tattoos sat glumly next to women who were presumably the mothers of their children but might also have been their own mothers—or their sisters or cousins or aunts. Everywhere there were children with women who were not their mothers but who had taken custody of them when those mothers got arrested or became otherwise indisposed. Occasionally there would be a physical altercation and an officer would have to intervene. There was a sheriff's station in the basement next to the cafeteria. There was paternity testing on the second floor. The courthouse was its own little planet of grimness and dysfunction. By contrast, I felt bright and competent.

And I took genuine pleasure in helping Matthew. He may have seen me largely as a chauffeur, but the truth was I actually had pushed for some changes on his behalf and thus solved a few problems for him. I can't disclose what they were, but suffice it to say they were the kinds of problems that a kid with a family would simply never run up against, problems stemming mostly from the fact that he lived in an institutional setting and was essentially being raised by committee. It was the kind of help I think I'd subconsciously wanted to provide for Nikki. I wanted to contribute to her life without intruding upon it. And deep down maybe that's what she'd wanted, too, when she signed up for all those mentors.

As it was, I always had the sense with Nikki that she'd rather be just about anywhere else than with me, even when she'd been the one to initiate an outing. One year, near her birthday, we'd been at the mall and she'd expressed a desire to celebrate with her friends by going to a certain movie on opening day. Unfortunately it was one of those movies that sell out before their titles even go up on the marquee, even if they're playing on multiple screens, and Nikki didn't have a credit card or any way of purchasing tickets ahead of time. And though she didn't ask me to buy her anything, I considered her plight and offered to buy six advance tickets for her and her friends. This would be her birthday present, I told her. As long as she was sure she'd be able to secure a ride to the theater and assemble the whole group with no one dropping out at the last minute. She said she was sure. She seemed happy as she tucked the tickets into her purse, taking care to put them where she wouldn't lose them. I was happy, too, though somewhat surprised at myself for impulsively forking over more than $100.

When I saw her a few weeks later, I asked how the movie was. She told me they ended up not going, that she and a smaller group of friends went out to dinner instead.

I didn't say anything to her. By that I mean I didn't say anything beyond "What? Really? After all that?" I didn't say the thing that even then I knew I should have, which is that $100 was not a small amount to me and that not using the tickets was disrespectful and inconsiderate. I didn't say it because I didn't feel like our relationship was such that I could scold her. I also didn't say it because she hadn't asked me to buy the tickets in the first place. Looking back on it now, I see that they were more of a burden than a gift. As much as she'd insisted that going to the movies with her friends was exactly what she'd wanted to do on her birthday, I now know that you cannot expect a teenager to plan more than one day into the future. It's hard enough to get adults to commit to a social activity until they're sure they're not getting a better offer elsewhere. But I suspect that ultimately what I wanted most from Nikki was for her not to act like a teenager. I didn't like teenagers. I hadn't even liked them when I was one myself. I wanted her to act like an adult, which as it happens was what my parents had wanted from me when I was a teenager and even a young child. So I didn't say anything to her about wasting the movie tickets. I merely reminded myself that this was yet another example of why I should never have children. Childhood itself was anathema to me. The very condition gave me the shivers.

I think in part that's why I was interested in foster children. In some cases, childhood had literally been beaten out of them. And though I had grown up a million miles from anything resembling physical abuse or neglect—if anything I'd been overparented, oversupervised, vested with far too many unmeetable expectations—the foster kids I met seemed alienated from their own childhoods in a way that felt familiar to me. Whereas with Maricela and Nikki the idea in some ways had been to keep them from growing up too fast, foster kids were essentially victims of their own youth. And they knew it as well as anyone. As much as they wanted to be normal kids, there was almost always a sense in them of wanting to get on with things. This phase of being a minor, of having no control over your fate and no say over what you eat or where you sleep or who's acting as your guardian and for how long, was a phase to be endured. No one ever said to a foster child, "Enjoy being a kid now, because one day you'll have to be a grown-up." It was no accident that when they aged out of the system it was called "emancipating." It seemed to me like the perfect word. What was adulthood, after all, but a permanent release from the chamber of childhood? Why would they have referred to these children as "minors" (in court documents, Matthew was never referred to as Matthew but as "the minor") if there wasn't at least some hope of major improvement down the road?

But that was my particular view, which was colored by my own particular experience as a young person who couldn't stand being young—in other words, a twisted view. It also doesn't really hold up when it comes to kids in the child welfare system, since the data on what happens to kids after they age out of the system without a permanent family is dismal. Statistics from the Department of Health and Human Services consistently show that more than half end up either homeless or in jail. Within two years of aging out of the system, as many as half of the young women will be pregnant. Besides, time moves at an excruciating pace for all kids. A month might as well be a year. On the days I went to court with Matthew, I watched child after child, some of them infants in plastic bucket carriers, appear before judges whose jobs essentially boiled down to issuing timelines. Parents were given six or twelve or eighteen months to get their acts together. They were told to go to rehab, to anger-management therapy, and to parenting classes. And when they failed to do so, the clock would start all over again. The children would hear this news and sometimes their faces would go jagged with despair. How was it that they'd been taken away in fourth grade and now they were in sixth? Sometimes they were afraid of the parents and secretly didn't want to go back, though they told the judge otherwise.

Matthew, for his part, was an old hand at court. He looked forward to it because it meant missing school and watching movies in the day-care area, where kids of all ages were kept behind locked doors as protection from abusive parents who might also be in court that day. Though he wanted to be adopted, he no longer expected anything to happen at his hearings. There were no major decisions to be made or battles to be fought. Usually the judge would just remark on how tall he'd gotten or how nice his hair looked.

•

Initially, I'd thought Matthew would grow on me. But though I learned to identify some of his charms—his facility with technological gadgets, his GPS-like knowledge of the location of every video arcade and big-box store within a twenty-mile radius—I can't say we were great friends. Not that we needed to be. I was never going to be his role model. I certainly wasn't a mother figure. I was more like a random port in the unrelenting storm that was his life. And that was enough. Matthew's lot was so bad that it could be improved, albeit triflingly, with one mini-pizza at a food court. A kid with higher expectations would have been more than I could handle.

I was comfortable with that admission. I was happy to state my limits. I was proud, in fact, to stand up and be counted among those who knew themselves well enough to know that they wouldn't do right by a child and that therefore the only ethical and, for that matter, remotely sensible choice was to bow out of the whole enterprise. But a member of a childless couple can only be as strident as the other half of the couple. And in the aftermath of my miscarriage, during those confused, angry months when I was struggling to understand how it was possible to feel so sad about not having something that held so little appeal in the first place, my husband began to say out loud that he wanted to be someone's father—or at least that he might not be okay with never being someone's father. He wanted to use what he knew about the world to help someone find his or her own way through it. He wanted "someone to hang out with" when he got older. That said, he didn't necessarily need the baby- or toddler-rearing experience. He didn't particularly want to give up his weekends for kids' birthday parties or spend half our income on child care. He didn't need the kid to look like him or even be the same race. When I asked if these needs could be met through teaching or mentoring or even being an advocate, he said he wasn't sure.

And so were planted the seeds of a potential compromise. Maybe we could take in, or possibly even adopt, a foster child. This would be a child old enough to go to birthday parties on his own, a child old enough that we might actually qualify as young or average-age parents rather than ones of "advanced age" (if I adopted a ten-year-old at forty-three it would be the equivalent of having had him at the eminently reasonable age of thirty-three).

Of course, the experience would be nothing like the typical child-rearing experience, but neither of us was after that, especially not me. Having never craved a child, I didn't crave the intimacy that came from raising someone from birth. This child could be more like a mentee, an exchange student, a distant relative who visited for the summer and decided to stay on because we could afford him opportunities unavailable back home. Of course, any child we took in would surely need intense therapy for years or even forever. He would have demons and soul-breaking baggage. But they wouldn't be Matthew-level demons. We would find the needle in the haystack that had Ivy League potential. We would find the kid who dreamed of being an only child in a quiet, book-filled house with parents who read *The Times Literary Supplement* over dinner. Sure, I would probably still be a bad mother, but I would be one according to such wildly different standards than those set by the child welfare system that it wouldn't matter if I dreaded birthday parties or resorted to store-bought Halloween costumes. All that would matter was that I was more fit than the teenagers weeping in the courthouse.

I knew this was 90 percent bullshit. I knew that it wasn't okay to be a lackluster parent just because you'd adopted the child out of foster care. A few times, my husband and I scrolled through online photo listings of available children in California, but we might as well have been looking at personal ads from a sad, faraway land that no one ever traveled to. There were cerebral palsied three-year-olds on respirators, huge sibling groups that spoke no English, girls who had "trust issues with men." Occasionally there would be some bright-eyed six- or seven-year-old who you could tell was going to be okay, who had the great fortune of being able to turn the world on with his smile. So as the Central Sadness throbbed around our marriage, threatening to turn even the most quotidian moments, like the sight of a neighbor tossing a ball around with his kid in the yard, into an occasion for bickering or sulking or both, the foster child option functioned as a pacifier. It placated us with the illusion that all doors were not yet closed, that we still had the option of taking roads less traveled, and, best of all, that we could wait ten years to decide if we wanted to.

Or we could look into it sooner. One day, while my nerves swung on a longer-than-usual pendulum between pity for Matthew and despondency over my marriage, I decided to call a foster and adoption agency. Actually, I told my husband to call. Advocates aren't supposed to get involved with fostering and I didn't want to do anything that might give the appearance of conflict of interest. He signed us up for an orientation and I told him he had to do all the talking. He agreed to this plan in much the same way he agreed to certain home-improvement projects when I suggested them, which is to say mostly accommodatingly though without tremendous relish. When we arrived at the meeting, I signed in using his last name, something I'd never done even once before.

"I've got to be incognito," I said. "Let's not call attention to ourselves."

There were about thirty people at the orientation. It was the most racially and socioeconomically diverse crowd I'd seen since I last appeared for jury duty. This agency was known for its outreach to the LGBT community and there were several gay couples in attendance. There were also a lot of singles, including a man wearing a dress, jewelry, and full makeup, though he'd made no attempt to hide his five o'clock shadow. We were each asked to introduce ourselves and say what had brought us. One male couple said they were deciding between adopting out of foster care and working with an egg donor and a surrogate. They both wore hipster glasses and one had on what appeared to be a very expensive suit. They sounded like they had big careers. A young woman explained that she'd spent time in foster care herself as a youth and was now ready to give back by adopting a baby. She couldn't have been older than twenty-one and was wearing a hat and a puffy coat, even though it was probably 70 degrees outside. If I'd seen her in another setting, for instance the public library, I might have thought she was homeless.

"I'm interested in an infant only," she said. "But also LGBT. Those are my main two things."

She wanted a gay baby. Or a transgender baby. No one in the room seemed to find this unusual.

When our turn came, my husband spoke briefly about

how we were just exploring things in a very preliminary way. Then I spoke about how I was ambivalent about children but that this potentially seemed like a good thing to do. I then proceeded to completely dominate the rest of the three-hour meeting. Instead of being incognito, I acted like I was back in advocacy training. I raised my hand constantly, asking overly technical questions about things like the Indian Child Welfare Act and the American Safe Families Act and throwing around their acronyms (ICWA and ASFA) as if everyone knew what they meant. I asked what the chances of getting adopted were for a twelve-year-old who had flunked out of several placements.

"Maybe this isn't the right setting for these questions," my husband whispered.

"But I genuinely want to know the answers," I said.

As the meeting wrapped up, the woman from the agency announced that the next step was to fill out an application and then attend a series of training sessions. After that, she said, prospective parents who passed their home-studies could be matched with a child at any time and theoretically be on their way to adoption.

Her words were like ice against my spine.

"We're not at that point!" I said to my husband. "Not even close. Not remotely close."

I suggested he apply to be a mentor for "transitional age youth," which are kids who've emancipated but still need help figuring out the basics of life. He filled out a form, again with the slightly bewildered resignation of someone agreeing to repair something he hadn't noticed was broken in the first place. The agency woman said she'd call him about volunteer opportunities. She never did. We both figured it was because I had acted like a complete lunatic. If the agency had any sense, they'd give the homeless-looking woman a gay baby before letting us near any kids for any reason.

After the meeting, I was mortified for weeks. I felt like I'd gotten drunk at a party, like I'd launched into some blowhardy rant before throwing up into a ficus tree. Slowly, though, I began to understand why I acted the way I did. The notion of adopting one of these kids was so discomfiting that I'd unconsciously tried to soothe myself by turning the meeting into something I could handle, which was being an advocate. It was one thing to look at the children in the photo listings and imagine which one might be bookish and self-possessed enough to live comfortably under our roof. It was another to sit in a room with people who were really serious about it, people who were going to work fewer hours or go out to dinner less often or travel less freely in order to have the family they had always wanted. And I knew we were not those people. We did not match the profile of foster parents—the good ones or the bad ones. We were not known for our patience. We were not ones to suspend judgment or lower the bar. We'd once entered our dog in a charity "mutt show" (ironically, of course) and seethed for days when he didn't even make the finals in his category, which was "best coat." I told my husband that if he was really interested in mentoring he should call the agency and tell them so. He said he'd try, but he never got around to it.

When I was Nikki's Big Sister, one thing I'd always noticed was that people smiled at us a lot when we went out. At least they did when we were in the various necks of my woods, like the Farmers Market or the independent movie house or my local Trader Joe's. I guess it made sense. She was a black

teenager and I was a white woman. Moreover, I was a relatively young woman. Both of us looked like we quite possibly had better things to do than hang out with the other. But
there we were nonetheless, and baristas and ticket takers would
subtly nod their heads in approval. The few times I actually
ran into acquaintances when I was with Nikki, I'd introduce
her as "my friend" and then watch their faces leapfrog from
confusion to curiosity to surprise before landing on (at least
what I assumed to be) blazing admiration.

"It's so amazing that you do that," friends would say when
the subject of my mentorship arose in conversation, which
rarely happened unless I brought it up, which I almost never
did. Though I put in the requisite time with Nikki, even taking her to a Big Brothers Big Sisters holiday bowling party,
which I think she might have enjoyed even less than I did,
there always seemed something counterfeit about our dynamic. Very few people knew I was doing this volunteer work,
mostly because in mentioning it, I felt like I was eliciting praise
for something that didn't actually warrant any. Back when I'd
been attempting to mentor Maricela, I'd actually gone out
and bought a Polaroid camera so that we could take photos
and incorporate them into a scrapbook made from construc-
tion paper and what was left of the glitter I'd brought in the
first time. This activity hadn't been my idea. It had been
among the suggestions listed in the Big Brothers Big Sisters
orientation pamphlet. Maricela had been less than keen on
the project, wanting to talk instead about how she needed a
new soccer uniform but her mother wouldn't pay for it.

Around that time, I visited a friend who had just had
twins. I picked up each of her babies, patted their bottoms,
and then put them back down. They were warm and soft,
yet still at that scary tiny stage. Truth be told, I love babies

when they're between about five and eight months old, and I told my friend she'd be seeing a lot of me when they reached that age. She laughed and asked what I'd been doing lately. I had a Polaroid photo of Maricela in my purse and I took it out.

"She's pretty, isn't she?" I said.

"She's gorgeous," said my friend.

It was true that Maricela was a very pretty girl. But I'd spent a total of about three hours with her at that point. The ownership implied by that statement felt almost obscene. On our second session, she'd turned to me and asked, "What's your name again?"

"You're going to be an amazing influence on her," my friend said. "She is so lucky to have you."

A few months after that, I met my husband. I was attracted to him immediately. As I've done with just about every man I've dated, I thought about what it would be like for us to be parents together. I pictured us coaxing our child to take at least one bite of peas. I pictured us shaking our heads in bemusement at her precocious vocabulary. But you're never the real you in the beginning of a relationship. Eventually things get serious and you return to yourself. And from there the relationship either ends or makes a commitment to its imperfections. Either way there is loss. That's not the same as saying either way you lose. It's more like either way you have to accept that you didn't go the other way. But that acceptance is itself a loss, the kind that if you think about it too much might cause you to go a little crazy.

A phrase you hear a lot in the foster care world is that a child has "experienced a lot of loss." It will often come up in the blurbs accompanying the photo listings. *Jamal has experienced a lot of loss but knows the right family is out there. Clarissa is working through her losses and learning to have a more positive attitude.* At first glance, you might think these are references to the original loss, the dismantling of the biological family. But most often they mean the child has gotten close to being adopted but that things haven't worked out. With Matthew I often got the feeling that the trauma of being removed from his biological parents had been dwarfed by the cumulative implosions of the placements that followed. He seemed to know that he'd had a hand in at least some of these disruptions, that he'd lost his temper too many times or let himself lapse into behavior that frightened people. But when I asked about this, which I only did once or twice, he tended to offer some standard-issue excuse on behalf of the estranged parents, which he'd surely heard from his social workers. He'd say they lacked the resources to sufficiently meet his needs. He'd say they didn't have the skills to handle a kid like him.

Matthew had been taken to a number of adoption fairs over the years, a concept that floored me when I first heard about it. These were organized events such as picnics or carnivals where adoptable kids and prospective parents were supposed to mingle and see if they liked one another. It struck me as a barbaric form of speed dating. But caseworkers insisted that the events were benign, that the point was for kids to have fun regardless of the outcome. The same went for a local television news station with a regular segment that practically advertised kids who were up for adoption. *Clarissa is a wonderful young lady who likes to play dress-up and needs a forever family*, the anchor would say. *Jamal has a mean jump shot.* Then there would be a field report showing the child "having a special day" riding trail horses or getting "ace tips" from a professional athlete who'd been enlisted to show up for half an hour and interact with him on behalf of some charity. This same news station also had a weekly segment featuring shelter animals that needed homes.

About a year into my work with Matthew, he experienced yet another adoption-related loss. A couple that had been visiting him at the group home and later hosting him for weekend visits had decided he wasn't the right fit for them after all. He'd been hopeful about this placement, and when I visited him a few days after things fell through I found him pacing around his cinder-block dormitory like a nervous animal. The prospective mom had given him a used MP3 player, perhaps as an unspoken parting gift, but the group home staff had locked it up for some kind of disciplinary reason. He had his Kindle, however, which he'd never used, and now he sat on a bench outside the dormitory, bending the plastic until pieces of the device began falling off.

"I know what a huge bummer this is," I said. "I'm really sorry."

"I don't care," he said.

I wasn't sure how to respond. Every possible option seemed inadequate, maybe even capable of doing long-term damage.

"I know you probably do care," I said finally. "But sometimes we care so much about stuff that it's easier to pretend for a while that we don't care at all."

The temperature was in the high 90s; the choke of autumn in Southern California was in full, scorching force.

The Kindle was practically melting into soft, curling shards as Matthew tore it apart. I thought about the $23 he still owed me for it and wondered which was worse, enabling his mostly consequence-free existence by letting him destroy it or lecturing him about how money and the stuff it buys aren't disposable. Both tactics seemed fairly useless, but the latter seemed almost like a joke. The kid's whole life was disposable. Like most foster kids, he kept many of his things in a plastic garbage bag so he could grab and go as needed.

Through angry tears, Matthew was now declaring that he was never going back inside the dormitory and would sleep on the lawn until he could live in a real home. He said he'd gotten mad at the prospective mom for not buying him something he wanted but that he hadn't done anything too bad. He said he'd kicked some chairs over but they weren't broken or anything. He said he just wanted another chance but they wouldn't give him one and it wasn't fair. After a while, I suggested he put his feelings in writing. Admittedly, this suggestion was based on what I would do in his situation, not what he was necessarily inclined to do, but it was all I could think of.

"Let's go inside and get a piece of paper," I said. "And you write down what you want and how you feel. I'll walk away so you can do it in private."

He agreed, which surprised me. We went inside the building and into his room, where blue industrial carpet covered the floor and a low-slung twin bed was covered with a thin blue blanket. He got out a spiral-bound notebook and lay on the floor on his stomach, legs spread slightly and elbows propped up as he began to write. He looked more like a normal kid than I'd ever seen him. I left him and headed down to the common room, where about six boys, some of them as tall and muscled as men, were sprawled out in front of a too-loud television. A staff member sat on a stool in the kitchen examining her long, freshly lacquered nails. I asked where the bathroom was and, without looking up, she directed me down a corridor that ran through an adjacent dormitory.

In that dormitory, I passed another common room, this one filled with younger children. They were seated at a long table set for dinner and they squirmed in their chairs and fiddled with their utensils and of course there was one kid shouting above the others and holding a basket of bread sticks over his head where no one could reach them. Unlike the boys in Matthew's unit, these were actual children, little tykes who looked in some cases as young as four and five. Gathered there at the table, they could have been tiny summer campers in the mess hall. They could have been Cub Scouts gearing up for their nightly eating contest, after which they'd go off to the evening sing-along and then their cabin bunk beds and, eventually, home to their parents, who would take both pride and sorrow in the knowledge that their children could cope so well with being away from home at such a young age.

But these children were already home, of course. There was no going anywhere from here, except maybe to foster families or, if they smiled big enough, adoptive families that may or may not have the resources to sufficiently meet their needs. I slowed my pace slightly as I passed the entryway. It had been a while since I'd looked through the state photo listings (the more time that went on, the more my online self-soothing practices leaned toward looking at photos of puppies), but seeing the small, open faces, the feet that barely touched the floor, the institutional food heaped onto institutional plates, I was reminded of the tiny spark of hope those listings once gave me. I was reminded of the small handful of kids whose profiles I'd looked at more than once. I was reminded of the few occasions in which the conversation with my husband about adopting from foster care didn't necessarily feel like bullshit or a pacifier but, rather, a viable antidote to the Central Sadness.

I returned to Matthew's room. He was sitting on the bed, reading over his statement. He handed me the notebook.

I want to live with ———— and ————. I'm sorry I got mad. If you give me another chance I promise I'll never get mad again.

"Will you give that to them?" Matthew asked me.

"If I can," I said. There was no way I could give them anything. The decision had been made. Later I would look back on this moment and realize that telling Matthew to write that note was the cruelest thing I could have done to him.

Sometimes I think perhaps my greatest wish is that one day my husband will get a call from a person claiming to be his son or daughter. Ideally, this person will be in his or her late teens or early twenties, the product of some brief fling or one-night stand during the Clinton Administration. My husband will be shocked, of course, and probably in denial. He'll say, "I'm sure you're mistaken" and "I don't recall the woman you're talking ab—" and then suddenly his face will blanch and his jaw will grow slack. It will be like that absolutely tour de force moment in the Mike Leigh film *Secrets and Lies* in which Brenda Blethyn, playing a mother who gave her daughter up for adoption decades earlier, meets the young woman for the first time and sees that she is black. With great kindness (with a maternal sort of kindness, actually), Blethyn's character explains that she cannot possibly be the girl's mother. But then she gets a faraway look in her eyes and is jolted by a long-suppressed memory, her face scrolling through several lifetimes' worth of emotion in just a few seconds.

My husband will have that kind of moment. And then he will tell me the news and I, too, will be shocked. Eventually, though, we'll both be thrilled. This new relation will breeze in and out of our lives like a sort of extreme niece or nephew. We'll dispense advice and keep photos on the fridge but, having never gotten into the dirty details of actual child rearing, take neither credit nor blame for the final results. My husband would experience the satisfaction of having a grown child to hang out with and be proud of when the occasion called for it. I would experience the satisfaction of not having to be anyone's mother.

Barring that scenario, I've sometimes thought my husband should donate sperm to a lesbian couple. They would live far away and send us photos every now and then. We'd visit sometimes and attend graduations and maybe by the time the child reached college age we'd have saved so much money not raising kids ourselves that we could kick in for the tuition. Once the kid was at college, my husband could get on the phone with him and help with assignments, lecturing him on comparative politics and trying to explain organic chemistry. I'd overhear snippets of the conversation as I puttered around our pristine, art-filled, and distinctly child-unfriendly home (perhaps there's a steep spiral staircase or a large malamute) and smile at the it-takes-a-villageness of it all.

If I learned anything from working with Matthew—and

with Nikki and Maricela—it's that no such town exists. I thought I'd undertaken this volunteer work because I was, above all, a realist. I thought it showed the depth of my understanding of my own psyche. I thought it was a way of turning my limitations, specifically my unwillingness to have children, into new and useful possibilities. I thought the thing I felt most guilty about could be turned into a force for good. But now I know that in some ways I was under the sway of my own complicated form of baby craziness. As wary as I've always been of our culture's rote idealization—even obsessive sanctification—of the bond between parent and child, it seems that I fell for a whole other kind of myth. I fell for the myth of the village. I fell for the idea that nurture from a loving adoptive community could triumph over the abuses of horrible natural parents.

I'd also tricked myself into believing that trying to help these kids would somehow put the Central Sadness on permanent hiatus, that my husband and I could find peace (not just peace, but real satisfaction) with our life of dog hikes and quiet dinners and friends coming over on the weekends. Instead, we continued to puzzle over the same unanswerable questions. Were we sad because we lacked some essential element of lifetime partnership, such as a child or agreement about wanting or not wanting one? Or were we sad because life is just sad sometimes—maybe even a lot of the time? Or perhaps it wasn't even sadness we were feeling but, simply, the dull ache of aging? Maybe children don't save their parents from this ache as much as distract from it. And maybe creating a diversion from aging turns out to be the whole point of parenting. Maybe, since the beginning of time, it's never really been about anything more than that.

•

Matthew got transferred to a new group home shortly after he turned thirteen. It was practically indistinguishable from the old one, right down to its proximity to the local Target. I took him there to spend the $25 gift card I'd mailed him, but when we reached the front of the checkout line the cashier said there was only $3.29 left on the card. Matthew claimed it was defective. He said he hadn't used it. On the conveyor belt sat several bags of chips, a package of cookies, and multiple boxes of macaroni and cheese that he wanted to keep in the kitchen at the group home. He hadn't even bothered to try to stretch his budget to buy electronics. There were several people behind us. I was afraid he'd have an outburst either right there or in the car so I pulled out my credit card and paid. I knew he was lying and I told him so. He said he wasn't. He said no one ever believed him. He said he had nothing, that no one cared about him or ever did anything for him. He said no one ever gave him a chance or cut him a break. He said everyone in his life was useless.

We got in the car and he ate his chips as we drove in silence. When I pulled up to the entrance of the group home, he gathered up his loot without looking at me.

"Happy birthday," I said.

"Uh-huh," he said.

He slammed the door behind him and walked quickly toward his dormitory, as though late for something. Dinner would be served at 5:00. At the old place dinner had been at 5:30 and Matthew was peeved at the change in schedule.

Back at home, my husband and I sat down around our usual time of 8:30. We ate some grilled fish. I drank a glass of wine. We looked through the magazines that had come in the mail, pointing out articles to each other while intermittently talking about our day. It was a good meal. The evening air was still cool but the daylight was beginning to linger. Soon it would be summer. Friends would start coming over to eat on the deck. After that it would be fall and what passes for winter. Then the spring would roll around again and we would still be right there, eating our fish and reading our magazines. Our conversations and our sleep would remain uninterrupted. Our lives would remain our own. Whether that was fundamentally sad or fundamentally exquisite we'd probably never be sure. But who can be sure of such things? And what's so great about being sure, anyway?

THE JONI MITCHELL PROBLEM

The Joni Mitchell problem is essentially a problem of perception. It plays out like many problems of perception do, under a cloud of insecurity that sweeps in on the winds of cluelessness. Here is a common scenario. You are spending the weekend in the country with friends. These friends are educated and possessed of that patina of coolness that comes from liking certain musical artists (say Leonard Cohen and Paul Westerberg and Wilco and Sonic Youth) and majoring in something not altogether useful in college (English or Art History or Medieval Studies—certainly not Business) and working at a creative and/or intellectually stimulating and/or do-gooder, socially conscious type of job. They read serious literature and hip graphic novels and when they watch TV (*if* they watch TV; even though it's now possible to watch TV without an actual TV, some of them still cling to the late twentieth-century smarty-pants posture of "I don't own one!") it's almost exclusively the high-end cable dramas. Again, their musical tastes run toward coy minimalism. Except when it comes to Prince. They all like Prince. They really hate Sting.

So you're in this house in the country, doing the dishes after a communally prepared meal, and somehow the subject of Joni Mitchell arises. Maybe it was prompted by someone asking "Who's the best singer-songwriter of our time?" or "Who's the best Canadian recording artist?" or "What do you mean Björk is derivative—derivative of whom?" And Joni Mitchell's name will be invoked and someone will say, "God, I can't stand her," and someone else will say, "Yeah, it's like she's yodeling or something," and yet another person will say, "Yeah, but *Blue* is an amazing album."

Before you know it, the proprietor of the country house will have gone to the record cabinet and pulled out one of Joni's records. This record will invariably be either *Song to a Seagull* or *Clouds*. Moments later, the room will be drowning in Joni's trembling soprano and aching schoolgirl lyrics— "Marcie in a coat of flowers / steps inside a candy store"— and someone will be yelling, "Christ, turn that off now!" and someone else will say, "I remember my mom listening to this," and the proprietor of the country house (who may be one and the same as the person who remembers his mom listening to Joni; in fact, this may be his mom's copy of *Song to a Seagull*, stashed away in the country house with John Denver's *Rocky Mountain High* and all seven volumes of the Firestone Christmas albums) will say to you, "But I thought you wanted to hear it. You just said you liked Joni!" to which you will sputter some jumble of "Yes, but not this" and "Never mind" and "Forget what I said." And you will insist that he stop the music immediately and replace it with *Sounds of Silence* or, better yet, actual silence. And later that evening you will lie in bed clutching your iPod and scrolling through the hundreds of Joni tracks that, in some cases, feel less like songs than an aesthetic nerve center. And you will think about the Joni Mitchell problem, which is the problem of either being not liked or being liked for the wrong reasons. And you will think about how you've been lying on your bed listening to Joni and thinking about some version of this problem for the better part of thirty years and how this in and of itself—the lying on the bed, the *thinking*, the unending emphasis on some problem or another—is itself part of the problem. And you will feel at once ecstatically connected to the world and terrifyingly apart from it.

But enough about you. This is about Joni and me. I realize the clause "Joni and me" has been written upwards of 10 million times, mostly in diaries with flowers drawn in the margins and in sonnets written in galloping pink cursive. I realize that there is nothing original about being a late twentieth-century-born female who feels that nearly every major life event (first love and heartbreak, leaving home, next love and heartbreak) was accompanied by a Joni song that was custom-written for the occasion. But I'll just come out and say it: The vast majority of those fans are not fanning properly. They think they're peering into the furthest reaches of the artist's soul. They presume the lyrics are confessional. They assume they're listening to love songs. They assume this woman who writes lines like "I want to knit you a sweater / I want to write you a love letter" is the mouthpiece for romance-crazed girls everywhere.

Wrong, wrong, wrong. Joni is the ultimate antiromantic. Her major influence is not Judy Collins or Carole King but Friedrich Nietzsche. Joni has explained in interviews that it was Nietzsche's epic prose panegyric *Thus Spoke Zarathustra* that rocked her world as a seventh grader (here's to the Canadian education system) and whose ruminations on the eternal recurrence of the same and the death of God had a defining influence on her songwriting. Yes, she was initially introduced to the public (by David Crosby, incidentally, who heard her in a club in New York and brought her to L.A.) as a delicate flower child who sang about broken hearts and small-town sunrises. But her roots were steeped in dark, dystopic soils. She worshipped complication, trepidation, and mixed feelings of every imaginable kind. Her love songs were less about love than about love's inherent limitations. Her narrators asked not to be swept off their feet but merely to find "somebody who's strong and somewhat sincere."

I used to think Joni Mitchell was a big influence on my writing. When I was a teenager, her habit of cramming a bunch of words into one line, plus the way her lyrics tend to start with small particularities and ripple outward into universal truths, lodged itself into my ears and wound up directly on my pages. That is to say, they put me on the path to being the writer who, as a college student, kept an entirely straight face while producing seventy-five-word sentences that included both "Dionysus" and "athlete's foot" (and used alliteration).

Now, however, I realize that Joni didn't shape my approach to language as much as my approach to my own emotions. She taught me the power of not taking things personally. She taught me that feelings can be separated from the self, that they can undock from our psyches and hurtle their way to the outer reaches of the atmosphere, where they can transmit not just our own aches and agonies but also the collective invisible passions of, if not *all of humanity*, at least a whole bunch of people besides ourselves. She conditioned me to appreciate the concept of *amor fati*, another Nietzschean preoccupation that has to do with taking a positive view of all of life's circumstances, including those shot through with suffering and loss. (Though possibly the real takeaway is that even if everything in life does not in fact "happen for a reason," it always has the potential to be mined for the sake of art.)

The conventional wisdom about Joni is that she wears her heart—or even her guts—on her sleeve. There may be truth to that, but she also siphons out her messy emotions and rearranges them into coherent ideas, making for a very finely tailored sleeve. This is not the technique of a confessionalist, though that's the rap she gets. "Save something for yourself" is what Kris Kristofferson said to Joni after she played him a demo of her 1971 breakout-turned-classic *Blue*. It's practically impossible to read anything about that album or that period of Joni's history without running across that anecdote. But despite its omnipresence, the story has always struck me as generic and anticlimactic. We never hear what Joni said to him after that. We don't know if she defended herself or felt embarrassed or even cared in the least what Kris Kristofferson thought of her record. (Four decades later, it's hard to imagine that too many people ever cared what Kris Kristofferson thought of anything.) But it's also a crucial anecdote in that Kristofferson's remark is emblematic of one of the central aspects of the Joni Mitchell problem. It's emblematic of the tone deafness suffered by many who fancy themselves discerning listeners. It speaks to the inability of most people to tell the difference between putting yourself out there and letting it all hang out.

Letting it all hang out is indiscriminate and frequently gratuitous. It's the stuff of paint flung mindlessly at a canvas and words brought up via reverse peristalsis, never to be revised or thought better of, always to be mystically discounted as "a gift from above." Letting it all hang out is an inherently needy gesture. It asks the audience to do the heavy lifting. It dares the audience to "confront the material" without necessarily making that material worth anyone's while.

Putting yourself out there is another matter entirely. It's an inherently generous gesture, a gift from artist to listener or viewer or reader. The artist who puts herself out there is not foisting a confession on her audience as much as letting it in on a secret, which she then turns into a story. That's Joni's entire modus operandi. She doesn't want us to care about her heartbreak. She's inviting us to think about heartbreak in a more general sense. Her best lyrics seem to orbit the earth (it's hard to avoid the space analogies). They start with a small detail, like a woman in a makeup mirror or a sparkling Christmas lawn display, and accelerate to bigger ones like rain or naked flesh or the wrath of prairie thunder. Then they hit on a few ambitious metaphors about the sky or ancient gods, and glide back down to the place where they started, where the woman in the makeup mirror suddenly has a wrinkle or two on her face. Whether or not the artist behind such lyrics needs to save something for herself is beside the point. The point is that she had something to say and is saying it as artfully as she possibly can. Whether or not there's anything left of her afterward is none of our business.

My interest in Joni starts in 1970 with *Ladies of the Canyon*. Admittedly, this album is hit-and-miss, as is 1971's classic, supposedly unassailable *Blue*. I know I'm committing blasphemy by saying that about *Blue*. But even though the piano songs are sublime—there's the anti–Christmas carol "River," the anti–romance ballad "The Last Time I Saw Richard," and, of course, the title track, which may well be a perfect song—the rest of *Blue* ("A Case of You" excepted) has always sounded to me tinny and unanchored.

Not that I don't think *Blue* deserves its vaunted status. The go-to record for dumped girls everywhere, it's rightly recognized as one of the great examples—perhaps *the* great example—of emotional bloodletting channeled into the cause of great art. I just think Joni didn't hit her stride until *For the Roses* in 1972. This was when her famous alternate guitar tunings started to get *really* alternate. This was when her records started to feel less like short story collections and more like novels, with songs folding into each other and Big Ideas looming overhead like weather systems.

I may be one of approximately thirty-four people on earth who genuinely like *Mingus*, Joni's rather minimalist and sometimes petulant 1979 collaboration with the jazz bassist and composer Charles Mingus, recorded months before he died of Lou Gehrig's disease. I like it because it does not spend even a millisecond of its time trying to make itself accessible to people who liked *Song to a Seagull* or even *Blue*. I like it because "The Dry Cleaner from Des Moines" is a tour de force of circumlocutions and syncopations. I like it because I'm forever mesmerized by "The Wolf That Lives in Lindsay," which has the line "the stab and glare and buckshot of the heavy, heavy snow." I dare anyone reading this to find a recording artist of any era who can deliver a line of such sharpness and elegance.

On second thought, scratch that. Waging such a bet will only result in a pileup of ineligible candidates. These candidates—Kate Bush (nope, too whimsical), Rickie Lee Jones (too train-wrecked), Bob Dylan (a decent poet but, sorry, not remotely the musician that Joni is[*])—will reveal not just the futility of my How to Correctly Appreciate Joni Mitchell tutorial but also the vast scope and many applications

---

[*]Likely to be the most controversial statement in this entire book.

of the Joni Mitchell problem. That is to say, they will remind me all over again that no matter how vigorously I tell people that no judgments should be made about Joni based on "Big Yellow Taxi" or "The Circle Game," country house record collections will always contain *Clouds* and *Song to a Seagull* and not *Mingus* or *Don Juan's Reckless Daughter*. There will always be people not just mocking the yodeling but, worse, *preferring* the yodeling. There will always be people liking things for the wrong reasons. No one knows that more than Joni herself, who told *The New York Times* in 1991 that she "didn't like getting to a place where my audience was bigger than those who understood what I was saying."

The thing with being a Joni fan, of course, is that it's always mattered less that we understood what she was saying than that she understood what we were feeling. I may be a snob about the tunings and the instrumentation but I was never above drawing all kinds of far-fetched connections between her life as a major recording artist and my life as a regular person. As it is for nearly all Joni-philes, this identification was especially strong in high school. In the tenth grade, for example, I was convinced that lines like "acid, booze, and ass / needles, guns, and grass" described my situation exactly.

Never mind that this lyric, from the song "Blue," supposedly expressed Joni's grief over the demise of her relationship with the heroin-using James Taylor. To me, the song was about a certain brooding burnout I had a crush on who smoked cigarettes on the front lawn of the high school (the front lawn, for some reason, was a haven for stoners and Ultimate Frisbee players) and who seemed to enjoy trading affectionate insults with me in math class but stopped short of wanting to be my boyfriend (maybe because he was *literally having sex* with an older girl from another town, or so the rumors went).

Other Joni lyrics that told the story of my life were as follows:

1. "Since I was seventeen I've had no one over me."
   Getting driver's license at age seventeen (legal driving age in New Jersey). Lodi DMV, this song's for you!
2. "You love your loving, but not like you love your freedom."
   College boyfriend number one.
3. "I guess you learn to refuse what you think you can't handle."
   College boyfriend number two, who dumped me because he was clearly intimidated by me. (Also applies to dropping Introduction to Linguistic Anthropology beginning of sophomore year after seeing scary syllabus.)
4. "He saw my complications / and he mirrored me back simplified."
   Jock boyfriend who had no idea what I was saying half the time.
5. "No regrets, Coyote / We just come from such different sets of circumstances."
   Mountain-man boyfriend who didn't know how to use a computer.
6. "You can't hold the hand of a rock and roll man."
   Also true of guys who work in finance.

I'll stop there. But, believe me, I could go on.

Unlike Joni, I have never referred to anyone as my "lover." As with the use of double negatives by ostensibly educated people, the word *lover* is something that works only in song lyrics. Otherwise you sound imbecilic. Unless you are Joni Mitchell. Joni has had many lovers, both in her songs and in her life. Her lyrics have her counting "lovers like railroad cars," marking time "by lovers and styles of clothes." Her curriculum vitae in the bedroom reads like a who's who of sweaty art boys of the Nixon era. She had relationships with David Crosby and James Taylor and Jackson Browne. She had flings with Sam Shepard and Warren Beatty and even Leonard Cohen. "A Case of You," with its "map of Canada with your face sketched on it twice," is apparently about Cohen. She dated several members of her band, including the jazz drummers John Guerin and Don Alias. For twelve years in the 1980s and early 1990s she was married to her bass player, Larry Klein, who was thirteen years younger than she.

Joni's great love is always said to have been Graham Nash, who was utterly besotted with her and wrote the Crosby, Stills, and Nash classic "Our House" about their life together in Laurel Canyon in the late 1960s. But Nash wanted to get married and because Joni associated marriage with her grandmother's thwarted creative ambitions (not to mention her own first very brief marriage, which she's said had her thinking, "How am I going to get out of this?" even as she walked down the aisle), she ran off to Europe and broke up with him via telegram. It read, famously, *If you hold sand too tightly it will run through your fingers*. Ironically, I don't think this line would have passed muster as one of her song lyrics.

"Joni is not a person that you stay in a relationship with," David Crosby said about her. "It always goes awry, no matter who you are. It's an inevitable thing."

·

In 2006 I met Joni. In fact, I had dinner with her. One after-noon in December I drove past an art gallery in Los Angeles with a banner hanging in front announcing "Joni Mitchell's Green Flag Song." At first I thought I'd misread the sign and that the artist must surely be the late abstract expressionist painter Joan Mitchell. But it really did say *Joni* Mitchell. Joni has always painted and she's always taken it very seriously, even if the public hasn't.

I was into the second year of my newspaper column at that point and it occurred to me that a Joni Mitchell art show might be a good thing to write about. It also occurred to me that this could be a good way to meet Joni Mitchell, which was far more important than coming up with a column. I visited the gallery a few days later and met the owner. He was an older Russian émigré who'd been doing print work for Joni for years but hadn't really known who she was until his son explained that it wouldn't be a bad idea to give her a show. Even now, he was not familiar with any of her music.

The exhibit was made up of a series of sixty photographic triptychs bearing green, semiabstract images. The gallerist explained that the work had come about when Joni's televi-sion set broke and began displaying zigzagging green lines and splotches that looked like photographic negatives. Joni took pictures of the screen with a cheap camera and, looking at them as a whole, thought they reflected the brutality and hypocrisy of the current political scene. Then she had the photos enlarged and printed on canvas.

The gallerist kept me there for more than two hours. He led me from triptych to triptych, explaining their meanings in a thick, phlegmy accent I could barely understand. I pretended to scribble things down in my notebook. I told him that what would be really helpful, for the sake of the column, was if I could interview Joni sometime when she came into the gallery.

"I wouldn't take up too much of her time," I said.

He said he was having dinner with her the next night and maybe I could join them.

"Really?" I yelped.

He said he'd check with Joni to make sure it was all right and then call me and tell me where we were meeting.

"We're meeting at Crevin's," he said the next day. "In West Hollywood."

"Crevin's?" I asked. "I've never heard of it."

"Joni likes it there," he said. "Because she can smoke. Dress warmly. We sit outdoors."

It took nearly an hour of searching for Crevin's on the Internet before I realized the restaurant was actually called Cravings. I allowed extra time to get there in evening traffic and arrived thirty minutes early. I sat in my car until five minutes before the meeting time and then entered the restaurant. The gallery owner was there but not Joni and we sat in the bar for forty-five minutes as he talked nonstop about "the passion of the art life." I nodded along, understanding about every fifth word.

"Ah," he said finally. "Here is Johnny."

She was a big woman. Big as in strapping, strong boned. She was tall, with big cheekbones, and big teeth in a big mouth. She was sixty-three years old, though a near lifetime of smoking had etched at least another decade onto her face. Her hair was blond as ever and long as ever and pulled back in a loose bun. Though I can't exactly remember now, I think she was wearing some kind of poncho. I'm pretty sure she was wearing huge earrings, although it's possible that her persona is so closely tied to the huge-earring aesthetic that I've just imposed that on her in retrospect.

We were seated at a table outside. It was about 45 degrees. Joni took out a pack of cigarettes. American Spirits in the yellow box. She explained that her biorhythmic schedule was to sleep during the day and stay up all night, so this was actually her breakfast. She ordered a cup of tea and nothing else. I was starving but I ordered a bowl of soup and nothing else. I got out my notebook, though it was too dark to see anything I wrote down.

We talked about "Green Flag Song." A few years earlier, she told me, she'd gone up to her house in British Columbia and taken a lot of landscape photos. When she got back to L.A. she discovered that her television had become "magical." She was very angry with George Bush. She was even more furious with Dick Cheney. She thought the whole administration should be tried for war crimes. Then she talked about how multinational corporations were not only destroying the environment and the world's economy but also tapping into the personal energy fields of every human on earth. She said the United States was on the brink of a major food and water shortage and that today's young generation, growing up on materialism and rap music, was not prepared to handle it.

She said the Internet was wasting untold amounts of electricity and that this electricity was interfering with the sonar of marine mammals, particularly whales. She spoke in a casual, matter-of-fact tone that suggested she was merely stating the obvious.

I bobbed my head up and down and scribbled random words into my notebook: *torture, energy fields, whales.* I asked if we might talk a bit about her music.

"Of course," she said, stamping out what was easily her twelfth cigarette and lighting another in one fluid gesture.

I asked her about the time signature changes in the middle section of "Paprika Plains," a lush, sweeping, highly strange sixteen-minute track on *Don Juan's Reckless Daughter.* Had she written or planned them that way ahead of time or did they just evolve in the studio? This was something I'd always wanted to know. She said they were very much planned but that none of the players had been able to figure out what she wanted. I told her how much I loved the "stab and glare and buckshot" line in "The Wolf That Lives in Lindsay." I told her that her music had been a profound influence on my writing. I told her that most of what I know about metaphor I learned from her.

I asked her about the Joni Mitchell problem. Not the part about people in country houses making fun of her yodeling but the part about people assuming she's sentimental and confessional when in fact she's the opposite. I said I always thought she wasn't a poet as much as a kind of musical essayist. Moreover, the lyrics people always interpret as confessions are really just invitations for the listener to come in closer. They're saying, *This isn't about me. It's not even about you. It's about the whole world.*

"You know what I'm saying?" I asked.

"Yes, exactly!" Joni said.

She seemed unconcerned that the ash on the tip of her cigarette was now half as long as the cigarette itself. With anyone else, it would have crumbled onto her lap. But Joni smoked with such authority, with such an absence of apology, that the ash sat motionless and obedient, like a dog waiting for a command.

"I'm more like Saint Augustine," she said. "He supposedly wrote confessions but really they were prayers for a fallen world."

I asked her how she felt when people told her they liked her early records but weren't familiar with anything after *Blue*. She told me that *Clouds* and *Song to a Seagull* were the work of a totally different person. She said she couldn't stand to listen to them.

"People get so hung up on the folksinger thing," she said. "They don't understand I'm a composer. This is composed music! It was the same for Mozart. Nobody understood what he was doing. They said there were too many notes."

Joni said no one had ever asked about the time signature changes in the middle section of "Paprika Plains." This pleased me immensely. Then she said that the political and social climate of the United States currently was a lot like Germany in the lead-up to World War Two, that Americans were not aware of the atrocities being committed by their own government and that the rest of the world was powerless to do anything but watch. She said people didn't like hearing this kind of thing but that as a Scorpio she could never help but speak her mind.

"Interesting," I said.

The gallery owner looked on the verge of falling asleep. Despite some early efforts on my part to loop him into the conversation, he'd followed next to nothing and had evidently smiled and nodded his way to exhaustion. I asked Joni if I might send her a copy of my novel. Not that I expected her to read it, of course, but given how much inspiration I'd drawn from her, I'd like her to have it. She gave me the address of her house in Bel Air and told me to mail it to her there.

"You have honored me tonight," she said. "People don't know what it means to honor someone. They think they do but they don't. You have truly honored me."

We hugged. This was an incredible evening. And the best part was that it was over now. The entire time, all I had thought was that I couldn't wait for it to end so I could go home and talk about it for the rest of my life.

The next week, the gallery owner called and said that Joni had read and enjoyed my novel and wanted to talk to me again. He gave me her telephone number, explaining that she didn't have a computer or even an answering machine so I couldn't e-mail her and might have to try calling several times before I reached her. He reminded me that she was nocturnal and said I should probably call her at night.

I dialed her number at eight o'clock one evening. Then the next night at nine and the next night at ten. There was no answer. Meanwhile, I had to write a column about the exhibit, or at least about something. I had no idea what to say. I couldn't make sense of any of my notes and I had nothing substantive to say about the broken-TV photographs. I came up with a column that was really more of an art review and my editor said it was unpublishable, not only because I wrote for the opinion page and not the arts section but also because I clearly had no idea what I was talking about.

I started over and wrote about my excitement at meeting Joni Mitchell and how I didn't know what to say but that if there was anything I'd learned from her over the years it was that if you didn't "write from a place of excruciating candor you've written nothing." I then went on to talk about how much I loved her music and what a great conversation we'd had. Except that I wasn't excruciatingly candid because I still half expected to see or at least talk to her again and I didn't want to say anything that would piss her off or make me seem so sycophantic that I'd be afraid to face her.

I called Joni's number a few more times, then decided maybe she'd gone out of town and that I'd try again in a few weeks. Then the column came out and I was so convinced she'd read it and been disappointed by its blandness that I stopped trying to call her. Several weeks later, I looked for the notebook where I'd written down her telephone number— the same notebook that contained her address and those useless notes—and I couldn't find it. I searched for it intermittently over the next few months and, in a burst of energy one afternoon, tore apart my office in disbelief that I could lose track of something as precious as the phone number of the person who wrote the score to my entire life.

But it was true. I lost Joni Mitchell's phone number. After everything—after the dinner, after the art exhibit, after the decades spent with my own private Joni as she piloted me through the indignities of adolescence and the indecision of early adulthood and the parting clouds of middle adulthood—I let the woman herself slip away like a dream burned into abstraction by the glare of wakefulness. Let me repeat that. *I lost Joni Mitchell's phone number.* I, *of all people*, lost Joni Mitchell's phone number. And also her address.

The column I wrote about her, which had the headline "My Dinner with Joni" even though we hadn't really eaten dinner, is one of the dullest I've ever published. It's also, to this day, one of the most popular. I heard from hundreds of readers, only a few of whom called me out for being so vague and noncommittal. Everyone else wanted to tell me how much they also loved Joni and how jealous they were that I got to meet her. Many told me how much they liked "Both Sides Now" and "Big Yellow Taxi."

I never talked to Joni after that evening. But in the years since, I've occasionally looked at the ocean and thought about the whales being blown off their courses, their compasses rendered useless by all the buzz and static crackling overhead. I've thought that this notion is most likely ridiculous but also strangely poetic. It's actually the kind of thing Joni would compose a lyric about. She'd be singing about some love affair gone wrong but then she'd go to the whales and suddenly the song would be about something else entirely. It would be about the difficulty of listening to your thoughts in a ca-cophonous world. It would be about craving silence while also wanting to hear everything. It would be about wanting to be alone and yet wanting to be in love. It would be about one of life's most reliable disappointments, which is that your audience, no matter how small, is always bigger than those who actually understand what you're saying.

THE DOG EXCEPTION

A week before my dog Rex died I submitted his photo and biographical details to a website called the Daily Puppy. As examples of oppressive Internet cuteness go, the D.P. is in the upper stratospheric reaches. People send in photos of their puppies, accompanied by descriptions that are often in the first person, as though the dogs have composed their own dating profiles. The goal is to win a coveted "Puppy of the Day" slot on the home page, a designation that invites a trail of gushing comments on the order of "Ooh, you precious baaaby!" and "You are so furrylicious I could hug you for hours."

The site also has a category called "Grown-up Puppy of the Day." One morning, as I looked at Rex and got the distinct feeling he didn't have that many mornings left, I gathered up a handful of his best photos—Rex on the beach at Big Sur, Rex in the flower garden, Rex in front of the Christmas tree—and uploaded them to the Daily Puppy's submission page, along with his (somewhat grammatically challenged) personal ad. "My name is Rex and I am a grown-up puppy . . . my humans say that there's never been a dog loved as much as me."

Despite an auto-reply saying that the high volume of submissions meant it would be weeks or months before my entry was even considered, Rex turned out to be the Grown-up Puppy of the Day the very next day. I was elated. This was essentially my version of my kid winning an Olympic gold medal. I immediately shared the link on Facebook, using many exclamation points.

As has been well established in these pages, such blatant displays of sentimentality are almost unheard of for me. My aversion to in-your-face adorableness, especially the kittens/babies/kids-saying-the-darnedest-things kinds that are endemic to the Internet, is so pronounced that I have been known to block people from my Facebook feed altogether if they so much as click the "like" button on a video of a kitten riding a turtle or a photo of some unwitting toddler sitting on his potty seat reading *People* magazine. But for every rule there is a hulking exception and the exception I make to my rigid antischmaltz policy is for dogs. At the heart of that exception was Rex. In his presence, my normally dry, undemonstrative personality flipped upside down. I talked baby talk to him. I hugged him constantly. I told him I loved him approximately eighteen times a day. I used words like *furrylicious*. I once entered him in a charity "mutt show" contest in the category of "best coat" and was incensed for weeks afterward (in truth: months, possibly years) when he didn't win. His face was—and for more than a year after his death remained—the wallpaper of my digital self-presentation: my screen saver, my social media avatar, the photo glowing on my cell phone. As I write this, the bulletin board above my desk holds five snapshots of Rex, one snapshot of my husband, and a couple of taxi receipts.

Though babies and children tend to elicit little enthusiasm in me, the sight of a puppy, particularly if it's some permutation of the large, long-haired breeds I favor, turns me into a swooning, drooling fool. I have been known to cross several lanes of traffic in order to fawn over some fluffy young Saint Bernard or Bernese mountain dog lolling on the sidewalk while his owner gazes into a store window or lunches with a friend at an outdoor café. These interactions, as owners of such dogs know, tend to embody the rather wincing combination of sweetness and awkwardness you see in interactions between children and people inside giant Easter bunny costumes. There's a soft, huggy vibe about the whole exchange that doesn't necessarily extend to conversation or even eye contact. There's a sense that the dog is both humoring the admirer and also very consciously performing a job. Having been on both sides of the transaction, having been the gusher as well as the human at the other end of the gushed-upon animal's leash, I see why pets can lower blood pressure and increase serotonin. I can see why dogs can do more for trauma victims than an army of clinical psychologists. They are security blankets for grown-ups, "comfort objects" no one expects you to outgrow. A fifty-year-old man who takes his golden retriever with him everywhere he goes is essentially no different from a five-year-old boy with a teddy bear. But a dog confers status on a man. It shows he is responsible and capable of love. It will probably even help him get laid.

I was an animal person from a very early age. And I'm sorry to say I was a proclaimer. My first foray into philotherian pride came when I turned seven and was allowed a Baskin-Robbins ice cream cake for my birthday. This was a very big deal, as it was the first birthday cake ever that had not been baked by my mother and therefore subject to her apparently irremediable inability to write on a cake. When we visited the Baskin-Robbins store to place the order, I made my selection among the thirty-one flavors (mint chocolate chip) and was then asked what written message I preferred. My mother had made it clear that "Happy Birthday, Meghan" was too conventional for her (and therefore also my) taste. She suggested I think about what other ways I might describe myself besides simply invoking my name. When I could not come up with anything off the top of my head she suggested we go home and think about it for a few days.

I stewed over this for nearly a week, cataloging my various attributes as though they were going on my permanent record. What was I? A second grader? A devoted fan of *Little House on the Prairie*, ABBA, and Nadia Comaneci? A reluctant piano student of Mrs. Dorothy Terhune of Pine Mill Road? The cake deadline imminent, I finally arrived at what should have been obvious all along. I loved animals. I had towering piles of stuffed creatures in my room (no dolls), boundless adoration for our cat, and a sensitivity toward animal suffering so acute that any picture book depicting even a moment's unhappiness on the part of an animal character upset me so profoundly that my mother had to draw smiles over their frowns or tears. And so it was decided.

"Happy Birthday, Animal Lover."

It wasn't until more than thirty years later, while sorting through family photographs and stumbling on that year's birthday portrait, that I realized the absurdity and borderline obscenity of the inscription. There was my seven-year-old self, wearing a pinafore dress from Sears and beaming over a green ice cream cake celebrating not only my special

day but also, by all appearances, my wildness in the bedroom. It also wasn't until then that I appreciated the extent
of my mother's generosity and her willingness to place her
daughter's wishes above her (quite substantial) fears of public
mockery.

Mostly, though, I winced, remembering suddenly the
rawness of my feelings for animals. I loved them too much
back then. This love got in the way of things. Every day on
earth is a minefield of animal tragedies, of baby birds fallen
from nests and insects smacking onto car windshields and
roadkill of all varieties leaving lumpen streaks across the
pavement. When you suffer from hyperempathy toward animals, the entire day can be an exercise in averting your eyes,
trying to shift your thoughts, holding back tears. But when
you're a child with this condition, when days feel like weeks
and roadside carnage is closer to eye level, when your natural,
childlike inclination toward anthropomorphization means
every squirrel and firefly in your midst has been assigned its
own little personality, the whole world can seem like the saddest picture book you ever opened.

So, as I got older, out of some kind of unconscious, self-
protective instinct, I began to wring the sensitivity out of
myself. Not all of it, mind you. Not even half of it. Not even
half of half. But enough so that I did not run crying from the
room when crocodiles sucked down zebras on *Wild Kingdom*
or when I heard aphorisms like "There's more than one way
to skin a cat." I did not shed tears when, at twenty-four, I got
the call from my mother saying that the last of our family
cats, Niffy Two (Niffy One had met a grisly demise under
the tires of a car shortly after that seventh birthday; wisely,
my parents shielded me from the optics), had finally died at

the age of at least thirteen. I traveled to Africa and watched in real life as lions ripped the limbs off gazelles and chewed until their manes crackled with dried blood and shards of bone. I even managed, in my early thirties, to live on a farm and cope with the brutality known only to those "lucky" animals that live in the country. The horses stood in the pasture through blizzards and hailstorms. Barn cats lived off mice and the occasional bluebird. A trio of Canada goose eggs by the pond, tended by both parents, who never wandered more than steps from the nest, was suddenly gone one morning, snatched by coyotes that had likely swallowed them whole.

Amid this carnage, I learned to buck up. I learned to care less, or at least to turn the pages quickly when I spotted a newspaper article about abused racehorses or circus animals beaten into amusement-worthy submission. But in the case of one species, my senses simply could not be dulled and that was dogs. Depending on their size and temperament, they were—and are—capable of delivering a joy I rarely accessed elsewhere. The mere sight of a doe-eyed golden retriever puppy or a massive, Sphinx-like Leonberger can temporarily alter my brain chemistry. To encounter a Great Pyrenees or a malamute feels to me like meeting a unicorn. That such creatures roam in our midst seems nothing short of magical. That such creatures might share our beds or lie on the sofa with us while we watch TV seems like proof that heaven is capable of dipping down and grazing the earth with the tip of its toe.

And there we have the sole exception to my antisentimentalism, my one area of unapologetic schmaltz. I love dogs so much it hurts. When I'm driving, any foreign object in the road, be it a plastic bag or a cardboard box or a disintegrating sofa that's fallen off a truck, produces a wave of panic brought on by my fear that it's a dead or injured dog. I have covered my eyes while riding in the passenger's seat, only to have the driver ask why I'm shielding my eyes from a garden hose.

I loved Rex so much that even leaving him at a friend's house for a week while I went out of town felt like a vital organ was hanging loose from my body. Once I read something in which a mother described her love for her child as feeling like her heart was walking around outside of her body. As a nonparent I'm wary of dog/child comparisons, because they essentially open the door for a flood of indignant reminders that the love for a dog is *nothing* compared with a parent's love for a child and that putting kibble in a dish twice a day is a *joke* compared with feeding/clothing/educating/shaping the moral compass of another human being for eighteen-plus years. So please understand I'm not making any comparisons. I'm just saying that Rex, the collie-shepherd mix who was my companion for more than thirteen years, lived with my heart permanently lodged in his gut. When he snoozed all night at the foot of my bed (and sometimes next to me, head on pillow, so we could spoon) I slept soundly in unclouded peace. When he rolled in the beach sand, scratching his back and flopping his tongue around as though having some kind of euphoric seizure, I, too, felt my every itch had been satisfied.

But you know what's coming next. It's what always comes next with dogs. Graying muzzles, creaking hips, tumors. To have an old dog is to look into the eyes of the sweetest soul you know and see traces of the early light of the worst day of your life. When that day comes there is no universally recognized ritual of mourning. No one expects you to take time off from work. No one understands that you cannot answer the phone for a week. No one likes it when you say the barbaric truth, which is that because pets occupy a sphere of uncomplicated, unfluctuating love, because their love actually becomes absorbed into the architecture of your home, their deaths can be more devastating than even the death of a close friend or family member.

I won't lie. Rex's passing was the worst grief I've faced in my life so far. Even weeks after the fact, I had bruises on my forehead from where I'd dug my fingers in while sobbing. Even when he'd been gone for nearly a year, during which time I acquired two new dogs for whom my fondness grew every day, his absence felt like a hole I was forever stepping around. I often thought about how, as a high school actress with desultory ambitions of growing up and going pro, I'd worried about my inability to cry on cue. In the era of postmortem Rex (and actually for months prior, when, despite his relative spryness, the mere anticipation of his demise had me choking up on a near daily basis) I pictured myself triumphing as an inconsolable, suicidal Ophelia, summoning images of Rex while flooding the scenery with a monsoon of tears.

But it was not just Rex himself that brought out such blubbering. Upon his death, as though enduring a series of aftershocks nearly as traumatizing as the main event, I had the misfortune of receiving from several well-meaning parties a copy of a poem called "The Rainbow Bridge." Actually to call it a poem might be pushing it. It's more like a pitch for an animated children's television show that's been broken into lines of verse. Except it doesn't even always appear in verse form. Sometimes it's more like a five-paragraph essay. Often you see it printed out in a fancy font on pastel-colored paper, like a morbid wedding invitation. On YouTube there are multiple video versions, many featuring gauzy footage of clouds and pastures and using the music of Enya, surely without permission.

The idea behind "The Rainbow Bridge" is that there's a vast green meadow "this side of heaven" where pets that were especially loved by their owners go when they die. In this meadow, which is also the entry point of a bridge that is literally made out of a rainbow and that leads to heaven, all sickness disappears and all injuries heal. The animals return to the spirited, bright-eyed creatures they were in the prime of life. In this meadow there is always fresh food and clean water and the sun always shines and the animals spend their days frolicking happily together, though they always miss the special human they had to leave behind on earth. Every once in a while, however, one of them "stops suddenly and looks into the distance." Body quivering, he leaves the group and runs across the meadow as fast as he can.

> You have been spotted and when you and your
> special friend finally meet, you cling together in
> joyous reunion, never to be parted again. The
> happy kisses rain upon your face; your hands again
> caress the beloved head, and you look once more
> into the trusting eyes of your pet, so long gone from
> your life but never absent from your heart.
>
> And then you cross the Rainbow Bridge
> together . . .

I try to avoid this piece of literature at all costs. Whenever I encounter it online or run into it in a veterinary office, where it will frequently be laminated and tacked to a wall amid pet-themed thank-you cards from grateful owners, I avert my eyes the same way I do when approaching something on the road that might be a dead dog. I do this not because the poem is bad, though it certainly is, but because by the third line my eyes will be glazed with tears and I will have to make a very conscious effort to shift my thoughts to something less personally upsetting than pet death. For instance, rectal cancer.

According to Michael Schaffer's *One Nation Under Dog*, a book I devoured a few years ago much the same way, as a teenager, despite never having owned a dog, I devoured *Your Neapolitan Mastiff and You*, "The Rainbow Bridge" emerged sometime in the early 1980s and has been published online at least 35,000 times. The byline almost always appears as "Anonymous," though several would-be authors have claimed credit over the years. These include a psychologist who says the poem appeared on a dog club's website after he wrote it for a grieving friend, and at least two authors of self-published books about the Rainbow Bridge, one of whom threatened to sue Universal Press Syndicate after it appeared in a Dear Abby column.

Over the years, Schaffer explains, the poem has been tweaked to satisfy certain gaps in its logic. There are Christian versions floating around that use scripture to challenge the traditional precept that animals lack souls and therefore cannot go to heaven. There are versions that retrofit the Rainbow Bridge so that it's accessible not just to especially cherished pets but to all living creatures everywhere. After all, how rainbowlike can a bridge really be if it accommodates the bed-sharing, carefully fed, bathed, and vaccinated animal companions of the world but not the millions of nameless, tagless, unwashed, and unbrushed creatures that die in shelters or perish on the streets? It would be like saying that the only people who will be reunited with loved ones in the afterlife are those lucky enough to have had a soul mate.

On the other hand, an equal-access Rainbow Bridge presents some real problems. Think of the overcrowding, the noise, the poop, and kennel cough. I imagine arriving at the bridge, fresh from my deathbed, only to wonder if the place I've come to is really a giant municipal dog pound—in other words, hell. What if I've been sentenced to an eternity surrounded by yapping Chihuahuas and nonrehabilitable fighting dogs? What if—and this part is almost too devastating to contemplate—Rex cannot find me among the throngs? What if he stops suddenly and looks into the distance only to lose all traces of me as quickly as he sensed them? What if I am left to cross the bridge alone, without Rex, like a traveler who's lost his dog on some far-flung highway, a lifetime away from any scent markers of home? This, of course, is worse than death. It's worse than watching Rex die. It's worse, I imagine, than dying myself. It is the absolute essence of abandonment. It's what dying alone would mean to me.

So, there, I've admitted it. The Rainbow Bridge poem makes me cry because as much as I want to never see it again I want even more for it to be true. I want Rex to escort me into the afterlife the way he ushered me through real life—at least thirteen years of it. I want to believe that Rex will be there when I die because, like anyone, I am afraid of death and, like a lot of owners of "especially loved" pets (though most are smart enough not to say it out loud) he would bring me more comfort than any other creature, human or otherwise, I can currently think of.

I suppose that's a sad thing to say. I suppose what I'm

really saying is that I can't connect with people, or that I don't want to, or that I'm unwilling or unable to do the work required to be someone for whom the idea of having a human loved one beside me at my deathbed is a source of comfort rather than ambivalence. I suppose it's even worse that this ambivalence can easily tip over into dread. Granted, like anyone, in my final hours I want to be surrounded only by the people I really care about. At the same time, I don't want to put the people I care about through something as disconcerting as watching me rattle and wheeze my way into oblivion. I know to some this logic sounds twisted. I know this is the opposite of how most people think—or at least say they think. I also know it's entirely possible—perhaps probable—that when my time actually comes I will see all of this very differently than I do right now. But if you asked me today—and if you'd asked me on any other day going back to that "Happy Birthday, Animal Lover" ice cream cake and beyond—I'd tell you that my ideal exit from this world would involve a dog at the foot of my bed and another dog (preferably Rex) running alongside me as I drifted into whatever state of consciousness lines the edge of whatever comes next.

I'd say this not to hurt the humans I love but to spare them a certain kind of grief. Not the grief of loss but the grief of performing the loss for the sake of others. Because one of the disadvantages of being human rather than canine is that humans are so often called upon to be phony for the sake of decorum. And the miracle of dogs—of all animals—is that they're incapable of phoniness. Even when they're performing a trick, they're doing so out of instinct and muscle memory. As much as we like to think they live to please us, the truth is they don't care about our pleasure. They care about getting fed and taking walks and not being left in a hot car. They care about maintaining a baseline of contentment. Which is precisely why they give us such intense surges of pleasure.

It's always said that pets provide unconditional love, but of course that's not true. The dog that is neglected or abused by its owner may try, for his own safety, to satisfy his owner's whims, but he will not love him, unconditionally or otherwise. Humans could take a lesson from this. "Unconditional love," as a term, rolls nicely off the tongue, but people say it without meaning it. The idea of loving someone no matter what they do is overrated, not to mention largely impossible. What is unconditional about dogs (about all animals, really, but somehow dogs have made an art of it) is their authenticity. No matter where they are or who they're with, dogs are incapable of being anything but themselves. Show me a dog that puts on airs or laughs politely at an unfunny joke and I'll show you a human in a dog costume, possibly one owned and licensed by the Walt Disney Company. Show me a dog that is sentimental and I'll show you one of those children's books whose frowning animal characters my mother had to draw smiles on.

And therein lies the irony of the dog exception. I may love dogs because they are so inherently without sap, because they are immune to manufactured emotion or self-engineered cuteness. And yet I express my affection for them in the most sentimental terms imaginable. I dump schmaltz on them by the truckload, cooing over my own charges in cloying baby talk, fawning over strangers' dogs in the park in the manner of a pervert casing the scene at a merry-go-round, writing Daily Puppy profiles in the first person and then slapping them on Facebook in a bid for the same attention craved by parents of toddlers who've mastered their mini-commodes. I'll wait in line for an hour at my neighborhood's annual Pet Photos with Santa holiday fund-raiser, force my dogs to pose with antlers on their heads, and then make custom cards using the portrait, which I'll later decide not to send out for fear of seeming pathetic. I'll then give in and send the card to a select few who I know will appreciate it.

What does it say about the human need for mawkish emotion that, when met with some of the least counterfeit souls on earth, when graced by the presence of creatures for whom affectation is simply incompatible with their DNA, we roll them in sugar as if they were candied apples? What does it mean that people like me, who recoil in the face of culturally enforced cuteness, take the placid tabula rasa that is the essence of dogdom and write all over it in loopy purple letters? I used to think such carrying-on was for people who needed to get a life. Now I wonder if such carrying-on is proof of life. How can we deny the urge to cover the blank spaces with our gooeyist impulses, to take the unknown and fill it with rainbows and wet furrylicious kisses? And what is more unknown than the contents of an animal's mind? What do we yearn for more than knowledge of what our dog is thinking—specifically, what he thinks of us?

Maybe only death is more unknown. Maybe the only knowledge more prized than a glimpse inside the mind of another living thing is a glimpse inside the end of life itself. And maybe that's because pets are, in a way, living embodiments of death. They guarantee us nothing other than the near certainty that they will leave us well before we leave them. They are ticking bombs that lick our faces. They are prescheduled heartbreak. They leave us no choice but to dread the Rainbow Bridge while secretly hoping it really exists. Our love for our pets is what separates us from the animals. Our love for animals is what makes us human. Which I guess is another way of saying it makes us both totally pathetic and exceedingly blessed.

ON NOT BEING A FOODIE

I hate food. Not that I don't consume it. Like any decent American I often consume too much of it. I just hate thinking about it. I hate shopping for it, preparing it, serving it, and cleaning it up and putting it away, though I would take cleaning up over cooking any day. Cooking fills me with a dread I can only describe as the sum total of every negative feeling I've ever had about myself. It takes my chronic impatience, divides it by my inherent laziness, and multiplies it to the power of my deepest self-loathing. For reasons I can only trace back to my lifelong inability to put effort toward things that don't immediately interest or come easily to me (a character flaw that has its roots in my grammar school mathematics career and eventually grew to include team sports, Middle English literature appreciation, and the proper application of eyeliner), my approach to cooking is not unlike the approach many people take when confronted with their least-favorite exercise in a fitness class. That is to say, I fake my way through it and hope no one's watching. I wait for it to be over.

I have never learned how to properly chop up an onion.

Instead of making small, radial cuts along the curve like you're apparently supposed to, I hack at it as though splitting a coconut. Dicing vegetables like carrots or tomatoes takes me five times longer than it should. Since I almost never read recipes all the way through before getting started, any prep work I deign to undertake is inadequate at best. I leave out ingredients. I botch the timing in countless ways. Since I have no innate understanding of flavor combinations or heat transfer and an utter disregard for precision, I forgo measuring spoons, ignore burner settings, and choose pans based not on their suitability to the task but on the degree of difficulty involved in extracting them from the cabinets or hoisting them onto the stove (I have absurdly weak wrists).

Sometimes, in an attempt to relax or simulate some magazine-spread version of "sensuous living" (barn-wood cabinetry, copper pots hanging like a Calder mobile over a butcher-block kitchen island, bottle of Shiraz sitting objet d'art–like on a countertop composed of handmade ceramic tiles), I'll pour myself a glass of wine and take grateful little sips as I perform my incompetent maneuvers. But one glass has been known to turn into two. Throw in an empty stomach and before I know it I'm cooking slightly intoxicated. Before I know it I have even less energy for the venture than I started with, which seems barely possible.

Like I said, I don't actually mind cleaning food up all that much, especially if it means throwing a lot of stuff out. There's something cathartic about picking up the greasy remains of a rotisserie chicken or a half-eaten tub of ice cream and depositing it in the trash. You are expecting me now to confess that I have an eating disorder, that I'm a binger and purger, that the reason I throw out the ice cream is that I fear the alternative is to eat it all in one sitting. But I don't have an eating disorder. I have a living disorder.

Food enthusiasts, when trying to determine if someone is a member of their tribe, otherwise known as a "foodie," like to ask the question "Do you eat to live or do you live to eat?" My answer would be that I live to avoid thinking too much about what I eat. That's not to say I'm one of those people who forgets to eat. On the contrary, there is no more reliable antidote for boredom or writer's block than a trip to the refrigerator, where, for lack of anything more substantial, packages of lox and containers of leftover Vietnamese takeout beckon like street hookers. It's more like I forget to taste.

I eat neither particularly well nor particularly badly. Most days I consume some combination of sprouted-grain bread, honey, almond butter, kale, tofu, Brie, dried fruit, prosciutto, and chocolate. I'm pretty sure I could eat nothing but Indian food and sushi for the rest of my life and be perfectly satisfied. I haven't eaten McDonald's-style fast food in decades. At the risk of sounding more affluent than I am, my definition of fast food is the prepared sushi sold in packages at Whole Foods Market. This is also probably my favorite meal in the world, even better in some ways than very expensive sushi at a fine sushi bar, which can be stressful and overwhelming and therefore detract from the experience. These packages cost in the neighborhood of eleven dollars each and every time I buy one, which I often do during a shopping excursion that involves the purchase of very little else (maybe a box of Popsicles or an organic lavender-scented cleaning product), I pass through a cloud of self-admonition that begins with guilt over spending too much money and ends with a mild panic born of one of the central anxieties of my life: that my carelessness and boredom around eating and cooking point toward a deeper pathology, one born of a more general carelessness and boredom about being in the world. But then I exit the market and get in the car and am pulled into some story or interview on public radio. I start thinking about health care or filibusters or the new novel by an author who's being interviewed. My anxiety abates. Unless it's a cooking show or a segment about the latest food craze, for instance the croissant-doughnut love child dubbed the Cronut, in which case I flip to a classic rock station and hope something great like Grand Funk Railroad's "We're an American Band" comes on.

My mother was herself an unenthusiastic cook. Some people whose mothers were bad in the kitchen compensate by going very far in the other direction. The *New York Times* food critic turned *Gourmet* editor-in-chief Ruth Reichl has written about how her mother's idea of cooking involved opening the refrigerator and tossing everything she could find into a bowl, scraping off mold where necessary. My mother was more the boiled-chicken type. Her definition of spaghetti was a plate of unseasoned linguini with heated tomato sauce dumped on top. After a few unsuccessful attempts, in the mid-1970s, to prepare fried chicken using Team cereal flakes and Wesson oil, she gave up on making that particular dish from scratch and, to my delight, began buying the frozen kind. The meal rotation in our house comprised roughly the following: Swanson's fried chicken, macaroni and cheese from a box (again, the generic brand), spaghetti, hard-shell tacos made with hamburger meat and refried beans, and boiled chicken with a side dish such as corn (which I liked) or peas (which I did not and therefore made a dramatic display of swallowing as if they were pills). In almost all cases, vegetables came frozen and desserts were prepackaged or made from one kind of boxed mix or another (cake, brownies, pudding, banana bread).

For what it's worth, I do not once recall ever seeing my mother do anything with garlic, shallots, or cooking wine (though did anyone use these in the pre-epicurean 1970s and early 1980s?). She never shopped at a fish market or had any kind of in-depth conversation with a butcher about cuts of meat. She never owned a fancy food processor or had any opinions about cast-iron versus stainless-steel cookware. And though that's surely not the only reason I had so little interest in accruing tips or learning to cook so much as one dish (she could have worked in the Whole Foods sushi department and I probably still would have shown no inclination to be her sous chef, preferring to stay in the den watching *Three's Company* until being summoned to set the dinner table), I can't help but think that her lack of enthusiasm had a significant trickle-down effect.

Especially since I was anything but immune to my mother's influence in other areas. As uninspired a cook as she was, she loved buying crockery and other tableware and held a personal belief that any shortcomings in the meal itself could be obscured if not totally overcome by serving the food in beautiful painted ceramic bowls. This is a philosophy I have carried with me. Guests in my home cannot be guaranteed a fine meal (though it will usually be decent, since my husband will usually prepare it), but they will get elegant place settings and flattering overhead lighting. If they bring a side dish in a container that I find unattractively utilitarian, I will quietly transfer it to one of my dozens of rustic-chic ironstone serving plates before we sit down.

In fairness, my mother had a vastly more sophisticated palate than her own mother. My grandmother's idea of salad was either a wedge of iceberg lettuce slathered with ranch dressing or overripe banana slices suspended in Jell-O along with canned pineapple rings and mini-marshmallows and then topped with Cool Whip. My grandmother made sandwiches with white bread (crusts removed) and spread Smucker's grape jelly on toast, which I delighted in when we visited and would then beg for at home. This was an affront to my mother, who asserted her cultural superiority by buying only whole-grain bread and Bonne Maman preserves.

As unreceptive as my brother and I were to such gestures, I'd long thought that my father must have surely had some appreciation for my mother's culinary instincts—if not the cooking itself then at least her efforts to improve upon the gravy-soaked meat and vacuum-sealed produce they'd both been raised on. But in my late thirties, I was set straight. I had occasion then to travel with my father to his hometown in Southern Illinois (eighty miles from my mother's hometown in even-farther-to-the-south Southern Illinois), where we stayed with an old flame with whom he was now having some version of a long-distance relationship. (Somehow I'd been wheedled into giving an unpaid lecture at the local community college; also, my father was being honored, along with a former Harlem Globetrotter, as a distinguished alumnus of his high school.) I was warned that dinner might well knock my socks off.

"She's a fabulous cook," my father told me repeatedly. "Just terrific."

When I was served a casserole made from ingredients I can only recall now as something approximating elbow macaroni, cream-of-mushroom soup, and Lipton onion soup mix, two things occurred to me, both revelatory. The first was that my longtime assumption that my father would have been slightly less unhappy with my mother if she'd been a fine cook was completely wrong. My mother could have been the Barefoot Contessa and he would have complained that the celery rémoulade wasn't as good as regular mayonnaise. The second was that this casserole was one of the best things I'd ever tasted. I loved it. Had I been a different person, for instance someone who could cook, I would have asked for the recipe.

Not that I could have tried it at home. My husband is an inveterately healthy eater—irritatingly so at times. (When he is hungry he eats *oranges*. More specifically, tiny little clementines whose peels he leaves all over the house as if molting his skin.) If I came home with elbow macaroni he'd assume it was to be used for a craft project, which says a lot because crafts are another thing I don't do. His mother is a fine cook who bakes from scratch and has in-depth conversations with the butcher. When my husband goes food shopping he comes back with fresh produce and enough ingredients for several meals. Unlike me, he does not panic the moment he sets foot in the store, only to toss a container of overpriced berries into the basket before taking refuge in the nonfood aisles, where the displays of toilet paper and dishwashing detergents have a strangely calming effect. My husband does much of the cooking in our house and it is, for the most part, tasty and healthful. Though he is not a foodie, he likes to try new recipes, especially dishes from Southeast Asia and even Africa. Unlike me, he gets out the spices and measures them ahead of time so they're ready when he needs them. Unlike me, he reads the recipe all the way through before starting.

Once or twice my husband has suggested we take a cooking class together. From my reaction, you would think he'd proposed that we volunteer to pick up trash alongside the highway. I told him it sounded miserable. It would be pointless. My mind would wander within the first five minutes of the class. He'd be there measuring flour with the precision of a crystal meth cook and developing little in-jokes with other students and I'd be daydreaming about going home and watching *Downton Abbey*. More likely, I'd be dreaming of *living* at Downton Abbey. Flu epidemics and abysmal women's rights aside, I often think living in a Jacobethan mansion in the early twentieth century and having my meals cooked and served by professionals would suit me just fine. That's pretty preposterous, however. In reality it would be a nightmare. In reality I would be so intimidated by the servants and so awkward in their presence that the relief of not having to cook would be dwarfed by the pressure to make polite conversation. I'd end up taking dinner in my bedroom every night, like a grieving widow or an unseemly visiting artist. No, the ideal scenario for me is probably a meals-on-wheels kind of situation. I can only look forward to the day when I am a lonely, shriveled shut-in receiving regular visits from some grim-faced volunteer who comes regularly to my door with a cream-of-mushroom casserole garnished with Lipton onion soup mix.*

As depressing as it is to imagine my final years spent eating casseroles from an E-Z Foil pan, there's also something perversely comforting about it. Maybe because no matter how

---

*Mad from isolation, I'll be begging the volunteer, no doubt some overscheduled high school student who needs charity work on his résumé, to stay awhile and watch old episodes of *Downton*. I'll be jawing on about my younger days, regaling him with grossly exaggerated war stories from magazine journalism in the swashbuckling 1990s—"They sent an *intern* to Paris to interview Karl Lagerfeld—on the *Concorde!*"

far you branch out from the family tree, palate turns out to be as heritable a trait as eye color. Or maybe it's just because Lipton onion soup mix, as a garnish as well as a seasoning, is highly underrated. Besides, I'll tell you what's highly overrated: the idea of going outside your comfort zone. And not just when it comes to food.

"The comfort zone is a dangerous place, a dark abyss where anyone who remains there for too long loses his or herself entirely . . . staying within your comfort zone is giving up on life."

I read this recently in a "news" item entitled "Twenty Things That Mentally Strong People Don't Do." (Clicking on such headlines is another thing mentally strong people don't do.) The item, which appeared in an online publication that dubbed itself "The Voice of Generation Y," was essentially a list of psychologically unhealthy habits, including "dwelling in the past," "avoiding change," and "being misunderstood." As a practitioner of all of the above, I was initially alarmed. Then I realized that as a member of Generation X none of it applied to me, since for us dwelling in the past and being misunderstood have never been seen as signs of mental weakness as much as reasons to start an underground magazine.

Please understand that I'm not opposed to hard work. I know that, aside from winning the lottery, there is no such thing as success without hard work—though we mustn't forget that winning the lottery requires playing the lottery, which requires paying regular visits to bodegas or 7-Elevens, which is its own kind of immiserating task. But having lived most of my life firmly within the confines of a very specific set of interests and abilities, I can tell you that the comfort zone has many upsides. It may be associated with sloth and cowardice and any number of paralyzing, irrational phobias. It may be a dark abyss where misunderstood people lie around in fading recliners listening to outdated music. But I'm convinced that, when handled responsibly, the comfort zone can be as useful and productive as a well-oiled industrial zone. I am convinced that excellence comes not from overcoming limitations but from embracing them. At least that's what I'd say if I were delivering a TED Talk. I'd never say such a douchy thing in private conversation.

I once interviewed the actress Diane Keaton about her status as a "style icon." If you follow such things, you probably know that the menswear that helped make Keaton famous in *Annie Hall* has evolved over the decades into a wardrobe that has branded her, if not exactly a trendsetter, at least an unapologetic marcher to her own sartorial drummer. Keaton wears a lot of wide cinched belts and oversized jackets. She never wears evening gowns, not even at the Oscars, but she often wears elbow-length gloves—"It's just a little something extra," she said to me. When I asked her what inspired these choices she told me that everything she wears is an effort to compensate for some flaw. She said she started wearing big jackets to draw attention away from her narrow shoulders. She said she had "no waist" so she faked one with wide, dramatic belts.

In other words, Keaton only wears clothes that she feels she looks good in. And because these turn out to be very particular clothes, she ends up adhering to the same basic style no matter what the occasion. She's been anointed a "style icon" not because she is especially daring but because she has a limited range. It is within the confines of the comfort zone that she has found greatness.

What I take from this is that the path of least resistance has a lot going for it. The comfort zone isn't where you lose yourself. It's where you find yourself. Though I probably shouldn't admit this, the activities and pursuits in which I've achieved any measure of success are, without exception, activities and pursuits that came easily to me from the beginning—for instance, writing and speaking in the English language (not much else). Just about everything I started off doing badly I've remained bad at because I never really bothered to work at it.

This is an unflattering, even un-American thing to cop to. Of the many unattractive qualities I reveal about myself in this book, I suspect few if any will ruffle as many feathers as that one. If you are an adult of relatively sound mind and body, cavalier statements about not wanting to do anything difficult are basically tantamount to saying you're not going to bathe because it's such a pain to wait around for the tub to fill. But, while I'm not proud of the scale of my ineptitude, the truth is that I've gotten along pretty nicely in life avoiding things I don't naturally do well. And, believe me, these things are legion. These things are at least 90 percent of things in the world. Here are just a few:

1. Do math above a tenth-grade level
2. Program radio station presets in the car
3. Ski/snowboard/surf/hang glide/rock climb/ spelunk/anything involving bungee cord
4. Get through Chaucer
5. Cook (as we've established)
6. Wink (True; I physically cannot wink.)

As embarrassed as I am by these deficiencies, they are not my greatest shame. My greatest shame comes from the vast vault of things I do not *want* to do. Many of these things fall into what most people would consider the category of fun or at least potentially relaxing. Again, this list is truncated in the extreme. I could probably fill every page of this book with nothing but examples in this vein. But here are a few that come immediately to mind:

1. Play games (sports, board games, or otherwise)
2. Ski/snowboard/surf/hang glide/rock climb/spelunk/anything involving bungee cord
3. Go shopping
4. Go on vacations
5. Massages
6. Meal preparation of any kind

Note the crossover here. I lack both aptitude and enthusiasm for food, games, and leisure travel. Much can be said about this and much of it is totally obvious. My standing as a nonfoodie is merely a gateway into myriad other areas of noninterest. Clearly, I'm a killjoy. Clearly, I have problems with pleasure, with *letting go.* Surely, I'm an unhappy person. These are legitimate criticisms. I do not enjoy most activities that are commonly labeled "fun." Moreover, I'm weary of "happiness," both as a word and as a concept. Happiness is, by nature, fleeting—though obviously not as fleeting as joy. Joy is a spark, a sudden gust. Joy is literally *all about the moment.* Happiness has a longer half-life than joy but it's still not a distance runner. Happiness is a day trip, a short story. Happiness implies a certain freedom from doubt or regret or existential discomfort and is therefore impossible as a long-term proposition, at least for all but the most unexamined souls. Happiness is an effect of good news, which, like most news, usually rolls off our screens as quickly as it rolled on. If we're lucky, happiness lasts about as long as a decent manicure.

But *contentment*: that is something to strive for. My goal in life is to be content. By that I don't mean "fine" or "basically satisfied." I don't mean settling. I mean, for lack of better terms, feeling like I'm in the right life. Contentment, for me, would mean living in a place where I felt like part of a community, doing work that feels reasonably meaningful, surrounding myself with people I enjoy, respect, and in some cases love. It would mean spending as little time as possible doing things I don't want to do.

What I'm saying is that contentment is a tall order. Not impossible, but formidable enough to elude most of us most of the time. But there's a trick to it, a master key to all the dead bolts that lock us out of our inner peace. The key to contentment is to live life to the fullest *within the confines of your comfort zone*. Stay in safe waters but plunge as deeply into them as possible. If you're good at something, do it a lot. If you're bad at something, just don't do it. If you can't cook and refuse to learn, don't beat yourself up about it. Celebrate it. Be the best noncook you can be. When asked to bring a side dish to a dinner party, go to the supermarket and get the nicest prepared dish you can afford. If you're feeling poor, get macaroni salad. If you're feeling rich, get a balsamic roasted beet salad or some butternut squash risotto from a gourmet deli, put it in an elegant ceramic serving dish, and present it to the hostess with head held high. If she says, "This is wonderful, did you make it?" you can say, "I made the money to buy it," or "I made the five-mile trip from my house to the store." Or you can lie and say you made it, though that comes with the risk of being asked for the recipe.

Of course, for some people, being outside their comfort zone is itself the comfort zone. I'm talking about people who backpack around developing countries with hardly any money, journalists who become addicted to covering wars, and soldiers who become addicted to fighting them. I'm talking about base jumpers who put on "wingsuits" and jump from mountainsides and even helicopters so that they can glide around like flying squirrels for a few minutes and then very possibly crash to their deaths at 120 miles per hour.

Every so often, my husband will call me into the room where he's lying on the couch with his laptop and insist that I watch a YouTube video of "wingmen" soaring around the Swiss Alps.

"How awesome is that?" he will ask.

Ours is a mixed marriage. He says fresh tomato. I say canned tomato paste. He bakes pies from scratch. I am someone who, if I could pick one food to undergo some magical process wherein all calories, sodium, and preservatives were irradiated like tumors, would pick prepackaged cookie dough. Not homemade cookie dough, but the kind that comes in a sausage-shaped roll and has a slight chemical aftertaste. I love that taste. I love eating it raw, never cooked. I love that distant note of polysorbate 60.

Possibly until my early twenties, I thought "baking from scratch" referred merely to baking something at home yourself. If you had asked me, for instance, what cake was made out of I would have said cake mix. The thought of baking a cake without the primary ingredient coming from Duncan Hines was unfathomable. The idea of making frosting with butter and powered sugar instead of buying cans into which you can furtively stick your finger while waiting for the cake to cool seemed to defeat the purpose entirely.

Past a certain age, it becomes tiresome to blame one's deficits on one's parents. The fact that my parents eschewed just about every activity that was not related to the arts— "Just consider yourself lucky you weren't born into a family that goes *camping*," my mother reminded me more than once—doesn't mean I couldn't have devoted some part of my adult life to seeing past their biases and trying new things. Now in my mid-forties, I've been independent of my parents for more than a quarter century. That's considerably longer than the eighteen years I lived under their jurisdiction. I've had plenty of time to learn the difference between braising vegetables and blanching them. I've had plenty of time to learn how to make risotto or even carve a turkey. That I choose not to says less about my upbringing than it does about my innate recalcitrance. That I have found myself in the prime of life (which is to say early middle age, that evanescent period where relative youth intersects with relative prosperity) in an era of Cronuts and artisanal pickles is both sadly ironic and kind of sweetly perfect.

One of the great pleasures of trends is the option of sitting them out. Being a nonfoodie in a world of heirloom tomato ketchup and chanterelle mushroom omelets means saving time and money that could be spent elsewhere, for instance on Heinz ketchup slathered on greasy diner omelets. Being a nonfoodie isn't necessarily the same as being a picky eater. In many ways, it's the opposite. It's about not being discriminating. It's about being willing to eat pretty much anything. It's about being just as glad to dine on Lipton onion soup casserole in Southern Illinois as raw octopus in Tokyo. It means it's not necessarily a tragedy if you die before making it to Italy (not that it wouldn't be very sad). It means knowing your spouse didn't marry you for your cooking or your ability to pick restaurants. It means respecting food items that are too often denigrated and mocked: Miracle Whip, butter-flavored margarine, baking mixes of all kinds.

My parents were not religious, but we did celebrate Christmas. And every Christmas morning my mother served a marbled coffee cake that had somehow been dubbed "Baby Jesus's birthday cake." She'd make it the night before and my brother and I would decorate it with plastic Nativity figures, placing Mary and Joseph in the center to suggest a kind of holy wedding cake topper. I'm not sure how many generations back the cake went, but the recipe my mother worked from was in my grandmother's handwriting, where it was called Jewish coffee cake (my grandmother, who probably knew fewer than five Jews throughout her entire life, must have seen it as an exotic delicacy). Later, I worked from a recipe my mother had written out for me, though now I know it by heart. I can't give it away, but I can tell you that it calls for white cake mix, vanilla instant pudding, and a carton of sour cream, among other ingredients available not just at your local supermarket but also probably at your local 7-Eleven. I can also tell you that everyone I've ever made it for has said it's the best coffee cake they've ever tasted. They're right. It's really the best thing in the world.

INVISIBLE CITY

It's now been more than a decade since I moved to Los Angeles and I still sometimes feel, as I did back then, vaguely embarrassed about it. The very act of coming here seems like the ultimate cliché. Even if you arrive for the most mundane, non-Hollywood reason—to go to Cal Tech or to open a dental practice or because your pharmaceutical sales job has transferred you to Torrance—people will still think you've come in order to join the "industry." Or at least make industrial-size sums of money. People will ask if you've run into celebrities in the supermarket. If they're from New York they will be too cool to ask that question but not too embarrassed to fall back on the reliable chestnuts. How bad is the air? How much time do you spend in traffic? Have you gotten Botox yet? Chelation therapy? A colonic? How long did it take you to start calling everyone "dude"? (Actually, they might not know about chelation therapy—and neither should you.)

These refrains aren't offensive as much as boring, "too *on the nose*," as they say in television writers' rooms. They're like equating Texas with cowboy boots or New Jersey with hirsute wannabe (or actual) thugs in gold chains. Not that regional stereotypes aren't among the most accurate stereotypes out there. As easy as it is to find surprises in a particular locality (who knew Salt Lake City voted for Obama over Romney in 2012?), the nonsurprises usually keep a steadier pace. And this is perhaps more true of Southern California than of most places. From the gag reflex that is the expression "La La Land" (and its cousin, the equally odious "SoCal") to the predictable iconography of palm trees and luxury cars and fake boobs and Scientologists and pot dispensaries and illegal immigrants and "healers" of every possible sort, there are a million obvious things to say about Los Angeles. Many are just plain wrong, for instance the fallacy that no one reads or is interested in books. (It happens that L.A. has more independent bookstores than the brainy, twee Bay Area around San Francisco.)

But many of those obvious observations are right. There are a shocking number of people here who feel compelled to drive cars that cost more than, say, your average well-appointed suburban house in Dallas. There was for many years in the aughts a yoga teacher, beloved in studios throughout the city, who made a point of reminding "ladies with implants" to "be mindful of brushing too hard against your mat when moving through *chaturanga*." There is a vast amount of real estate in Hollywood owned by a church that believes its members are descended from space aliens. The surreal effects of watching these clichés play out before you in real life and in real time can make your head spin. They can make you feel like the one live person in an animated children's show.

I was born in California—in Palo Alto, where my father was working toward a Ph.D. that he'd never really need and my mother was effectively ruining herself for every other location in the world because nowhere else would ever be quite as perfect as the Stanford campus in 1970. I've been told that as a baby and toddler I was as much a part of the flora and fauna of the place as any native plant. I was blond and tanned (a tan baby! Can you imagine such a thing now?) and resistant to wearing shoes. Other than faint swatches of memory—a houseplant in a window, a giant sandbox in the married-student housing complex called Escondido Village, faculty mommies wearing Jackie O–style headscarves and hoop earrings—I have no meaningful recollection of the place. But I can say without hyperbole that when I arrived in Los Angeles nearly thirty years later there was a part of me that wasn't so much forging new territory as reclaiming an original stake. It felt like home even though there was no reason for it to. Moments of déjà vu would pop up in unexpected corners, as though traces of a past life were living inside the walls.

After Palo Alto, I grew up a little bit in Austin, Texas, and a lot in northern New Jersey. After college, I moved to New York City to live out the only cliché that's worse than the California cliché, the odyssey of the struggling young writer harboring naïve fantasies of bohemia. I stayed there through my twenties and then moved to the Great Plains, where I lived out an odd little prairie fantasy that mostly entailed drinking cheap wine and sitting on the front porch of my farmhouse watching hallucinatory lightning storms. This was something I could have done forever. Recognizing that fact, I knew it was time to leave. I could have moved back to New York, but I'd grown fond of my car and even fonder of my large dog.

It made sense to keep moving west, to find a good spot

in the vast parking lot that is Los Angeles. I was, coinciden-
tally enough, working on a movie script. During my time in
big sky country I'd written a novel largely about drinking
wine and watching lightning storms and it was now not only
being published but also possibly being turned into a film.
Somehow I'd convinced the producers to pay me to write
the script, less because I wanted to be a screenwriter than
because I wanted Writers' Guild health insurance. Though
this transaction had required a trip "to the coast" (there's
another cloying L.A.-ism; is the east coast not also a "coast"?)
for a series of meetings and a heady stay at an Ian Schrager
hotel, the job in no way required that I live there. I'm fairly
certain I could have fashioned myself into a far hotter, or at
least more intriguing, property had I stayed on that porch.
But I came anyway.

How many young essayists/aspiring screenwriters/liter-
ary people of any stripe have come to Los Angeles because
of that famous photo of Joan Didion with her family on the
deck of their house in Malibu? If there is a west coast equivalent of those seminal Woody Allen movies, if L.A. has an
Annie Hall or a *Manhattan*, which is to say if it has a fantasti-
cal, hyperaestheticized symbol of its appeal, it has to be that
image. Taken in 1976, it shows a sideways-glancing Didion,
winsome and tiny in a flowing dress, with perfunctory cigarette in hand and perfunctory gin and tonic (or something
thereabouts) perched on the railing. Her husband, John Greg-
ory Dunne, leans into the camera as though he's about to
disclose a secret to a friend sitting across from him at a bar
table. Their blond daughter wears a polka-dot dress and a wary
expression. Decades later we will learn from Didion herself
that these years were not all they seemed. But for now the

cliffs tumble idyllically beneath them and the Pacific Ocean seems to lie patiently in wait, a tableau to be either noticed or not noticed depending on the comings and goings of the day. The house looks modest, though it probably isn't. The deck wood looks salted and ragged, possibly unsafe for standing on. The photograph is in black and white. That's really the main thing about it. These people are living elegantly and (as is always said about Didion) *coolly* in black and white in a part of the world that often seems exhausted by its own colors. These people have it both ways, which is to say they have it all ways. Or at least that's the myth.

You could say I moved to Los Angeles in order to try to have a lot of things at once. I used to call L.A. "New York City with yards" but that doesn't really cover it. It's more that it's a place where wildness and domestication are forever running into each other. It's a place where coyotes sleep on lawn chairs and cross Sunset Boulevard in broad daylight. It's a place where bears dip into swimming pools in the foothills. I love that about it, just as I love that it's a place of invisibility. It's a place of tall hedges and private pools and driving alone in your car, where no one knows if you're crying. Los Angeles is where I learned that your ability to see is sometimes only as good as your willingness to go unseen.

Here is an L.A. story. Given some of the characters involved I suppose it could also be a New York story. But at the end of it I get in my car and drive home, which is pretty much the way every L.A. story ends. It's a story very much in color and also very name-droppy—in fact, it is in many ways a string of names and nothing more—and for a long time I was reluctant to tell it publicly. But the person responsible for it is, sadly, no longer alive to scold me for indiscretion. Not that she probably would have. She's the one whose motto (actually it was her mother's motto) was "Everything is copy."

Nora Ephron was a friend and mentor to me. I use these terms proudly but also loosely, as she was a friend and mentor to dozens if not hundreds of other young female writers of roughly my generation and sensibility. When she died unexpectedly in the summer of 2012, we all seemed to come out of the woodwork like mistresses at the funeral of a raging yet irresistible philanderer, churning out paeans to her in any publication that would let us and sizing one another up as if saying, "She took *you* to lunch, too?" Even before then, I knew I was far from the first rung of Nora acolytes. We had lunch a few times, once or twice in New York ("Next time I'll invite Joan to join us!") and again once or twice in L.A., where on one occasion she told me to meet her at Fred Segal and, not realizing it had a restaurant, I loitered around the store for twenty minutes before figuring things out and rushing to the café, where, to my great shame, I'd kept her waiting.

A movie producer Nora knew was seated at a nearby table and she introduced us. This was during the time when I was still going through the motions of trying to be a screenwriter, a venture Nora seemed eager to help with. Returning to our table, she said to me, "You are going to call him tomorrow and he will take a meeting with you and he will love you and you'll do a project together and it will work." She said things like this all the time—to just about everybody.

Anyway, this is where the real story begins. I did not get it on tape, obviously, so I can't claim to be telling it verbatim.

But I'm recounting it to the best of my ability, and if at any time I appear to be exaggerating, you can be assured that I am not. This was no cartoon. This was live action all the way.

One day Nora e-mailed and said she wanted to invite me to a party "for a games kind of thing." Though I loathe games of just about any sort, I of course accepted the invitation. A short time later her assistant faxed me the directions to her house, which included a map and also instructions to bring a written list of objects or titles or names that were linked in some fashion; for instance, *A League of Their Own*, *Field of Dreams*, *The Natural*, which are all movies about baseball. I spent no less than twenty hours working on my list, revising it endlessly, changing the theme multiple times, and just generally fretting about the party. I ended up with a list of rock bands that had birds in the name: the Eagles, the Yardbirds, A Flock of Seagulls, and so on. But that's not really relevant to the story.

When I arrived at Nora's house there were only a handful of cars in the driveway—a Lexus or two, a Range Rover, some BMWs—and very few parked on the street. This surprised me, as I assumed it would be a large gathering. Otherwise, why in the world would I have made the cut? I rang the doorbell and Nora answered, greeting me warmly as always. Though she lived most of the time in New York, she was in L.A. directing the movie *Bewitched*, and the house, which I think she was renting with her husband, Nick Pileggi, was grand if also fairly modest in scale—a baby grand. She showed me into the living room, where about twenty people, drinks and hors d'oeuvres in hand, were standing around in small conversational huddles.

These people included the following: Nicole Kidman,

Meg Ryan, Steve Martin, Rob Reiner, Larry David, Arianna Huffington, and David Geffen. Others included the spouses or partners of these people, for instance Laurie David, who was still married to Larry at the time, and Steve Martin's lovely young girlfriend and future wife, the former *New Yorker* fact-checker Anne Stringfield. There was a smattering of various producers and moguls I didn't recognize, plus, of course, Nick Pileggi, a famed author and screenwriter in his own right. There was also a small dog, and some stealth hired hands in the kitchen.

Nora introduced me to Nicole Kidman. The way she did this was to say, "Nicole, this is Meghan Daum. Meghan, this is Nicole Kidman."

Then she brought me over to Rob Reiner and did the same thing. Another guest pulled her away and I was left standing there with Rob Reiner, who seemed to be listing to the side in an effort to return to his previous conversation. He said nothing to me. I couldn't think of one appropriate thing to say to him. Obviously I couldn't ask what he did for a living or how he knew Nora. Everyone in the world knew he was a famous director and anyone with a scintilla of movie trivia knowledge knew that he went back with Nora at least as far as *When Harry Met Sally*, for which she wrote the script.

"Do you live nearby?" I asked finally.

"Kind of," he said.

"Have any trouble getting here?"

"No," he said.

We stood there a little longer. Rob Reiner didn't ask if I lived nearby or how I knew Nora or what I did for a living. He asked me nothing. I excused myself to get a drink.

Clutching my wine, I scanned the room for anyone

remotely approachable. Steve Martin. I walked over and said hello. More precisely, I walked over and said hello to Anne, who then made it okay to say hello to Steve. He was friendlier than Rob Reiner, though no doubt this was because of Anne, who I'd never met but who at least occupied the same social galaxy as I did—or at least she had before she went and realized the fantasy of every woman who ever majored in English or worked in publishing: to land a major movie star who also plays the banjo and writes Shouts and Murmurs columns for *The New Yorker*.

Steve Martin had a weird little mustache. It turned out he was in the middle of shooting a remake of *The Pink Panther*, playing Inspector Clouseau, and couldn't shave it off. Larry David was standing with him and I tried to talk to him, too, but his gaze soon shifted to some person or object behind me, registering the bored irritation of a wedding guest trapped next to someone's mentally ill relative.

Mercifully, Nora clanked a glass and announced that dinner was ready. She'd cooked everything herself: baked ham and green beans and salad. The food sat on the kitchen counter in giant aluminum pans and we were instructed to file through and serve ourselves. Out in the main room, the seating was haphazard, with guests spread out over several tables that had been pushed together at strange angles. The spots were getting snapped up rapidly and I grabbed one where I could, which turned out to be next to Meg Ryan. We said hello with maximum brevity and she proceeded to start a conversation with the guy on the other side of me. Like just about everyone else, they were talking politics. Weeks earlier, George W. Bush had been elected to a second term. They were very distraught about this. At the other end of the table, Rob Reiner was booming with indignation about voting booth fraud.

Arianna Huffington was gesturing wildly as though debating someone on a talk show. Meg Ryan and her friend were in deep discussion about how best to go after the Bush administration for war crimes. When I piped up, if only to lessen the awkwardness of our seating arrangement, they gave no indication of hearing me.

I never thought I'd say this, but the words "now we're going to divide into teams and play charades" filled me with indescribable relief. Nora told us to get out our lists and drop them in a hat that was being passed around. Then she explained that this was a special kind of charades called "running charades."

"It's much more fun than regular charades," she said.

"So what you're saying, then," said Steve Martin, "is that it's *sort of* fun." He said this neither loudly nor quietly, though few seemed to hear him in any case.

We broke into teams, each of which was assigned a captain. Rob Reiner was ours and he explained the rules, which essentially involved trying to elicit as many correct answers as quickly as possible. The clues were the lists, meaning someone would stand up and act out every item on it—the Eagles, the Yardbirds, A Flock of Seagulls—until the theme was identified. Then they'd move on to another list. The first team to work through all the lists was the winner.

Rob Reiner was a taskmaster. "Let's go! *Let's go!*" he bellowed while we flailed around trying to convey titles such as *The Kiss of the Spider Woman* and *The Crying Game* (it seemed almost everyone had brought in lists of movies) only to be met with shouts of *"A Beautiful Mind!"* and *"Boogie Nights!"* I couldn't help but notice that Anne and I and a few of the other nonactors were in heavier pantomime rotation than the professional performers in the room, namely Nicole Kidman, who had confessed early on that charades "is not my forté" and was now sitting on an ottoman in the corner, seemingly trying to avoid notice. Which is of course a fruitless endeavor if you are Nicole Kidman.

I need to pause now to say a few things about Nicole Kidman. First of all, she is stunningly beautiful. She is beautiful in a nonhuman way. She is an ethereal willow tree of a woman, with skin by Vermeer and hair by Botticelli. The other celebrities were of course also much better-looking than normal people. Arianna Huffington was tall and sleek in jeans and a crisp shirt. David Geffen, who I couldn't think of as anything but the "Free Man in Paris," after the song Joni Mitchell wrote about him, was fit and tan and affable-looking. But Nicole Kidman was in another league entirely. Her flawless skin was dusted with flawlessly applied makeup, her hair a cascade of shiny blondness that managed to be at once tousled and perfectly in place. If she didn't also happen to look very real, you'd think she must be fake—she was that gorgeous.

The second thing I need to say about Nicole Kidman is that I actually had a connection to her. I actually *had business* with her. The novel I'd published based on my prairie adventure, the one for which I'd written the screenplay, had been sent to various actresses to gauge their interest in attaching themselves to the project. Nicole Kidman, apparently, was among those actresses and apparently she liked the book. In fact, she didn't just like it. She was, I'd been told, "madly in love" with it, not least of all because the narrator's relationship with a soulful if substance-abusing redneck "resonated" with her vis-à-vis her marriage to a certain country star who'd entered drug rehab not long after their wedding. Though the project had been on the usual Hollywood stop-and-go course for more than a year, my agent regularly placated me with assurances along the lines of "Nicole wants to meet you" and "Nicole feels a kinship with you" and even, mind-blowingly, "Nicole wants to play you in the movie." By "you" they meant the character in the novel that was loosely based on me, a character who happened not to be anything close to a willowy Vermeer. But all that could be worked out later.

And now here we were. And as confused as I was about how to comport myself at this party, one unspoken rule seemed crystal clear: *Do not talk about business.* Even though, I was beginning to realize, this was in many ways a business party—Nora was directing *Bewitched*, which Nicole Kidman was starring in—I had not heard a single word exchanged about deals or pitches or award contenders or agents. It was clearly uncouth to so much as ask someone about his job, much less try to get them to play you in a movie.

So, excruciating as it was, there was no way I could walk up to Nicole Kidman and tell her who I was (clearly my name alone had not rung a bell). Such a move, at the very least, would have been disrespectful to Nora, who by invit-ing me to this party was showing she trusted me not to be-have like a starstruck careerist. At the worst, it would have produced the awkward moment to trump all other awkward moments of the night. Nicole Kidman would have looked down at me, a stranger easily six inches shorter with cropped hair and skin splotched in the places the sunscreen missed, and thought, I'm *going to play* you?

So, I said nothing. As the evening wore on I said less and less to anyone, not out of insecurity but actually out of a strange peace. I entered a kind of zen space, a pact with my ego in which I realized that, as bizarre and slightly awful as this evening was, it was also a dream come true. I was, in effect, invisible. I was the human embodiment of a fly on the wall. Who among us has not wished for that experience? How many of us wonder what it would be like, if only for an hour or two, to observe a situation both in person and at a vast distance? A situation, no less, involving movie stars waving their hands around while people shouted, *"The French Lieutenant's Woman!" "Grease!" "Schindler's List!"*

One problem with the charades game, at least among our team, was that no one listened to anyone and therefore when someone did call out the right answer it often went unrecognized. This happened to me as I yelled *"Gorky Park"* at least three times until Steve Martin spoke on my behalf and the message was received. The event dragged on and on, Rob Reiner and Larry David growing so impatient with many of the players that they finally gave in and assumed the bulk of the evening's remaining pantomime duties.

"I don't know what this is!" Larry David said, looking at a clue and throwing up his hands as if it were written in hieroglyphics. I thought for a moment that he'd gotten my list and didn't know where to start with the Yardbirds, but that was impossible since we were only using lists supplied by members of other teams.

Larry David began jumping around, stomping on the floor and covering his ears as though shielding them from a loud noise.

"Flashdance," we cried out. *"Footloose!"*

"All That Jazz!" Rob Reiner roared. *"Arthur! My Left Foot, Close Encounters of the Third Kind!* Come on, people! Just keep them coming! *Let's go!"*

Finally, someone got "thunder."

Blue Thunder? Rolling Thunder? Thunder Heart? Mad Max Beyond Thunderdome?

Then, at last, *Days of Thunder.*

"Yes!" said Larry David. "Though I don't know what that is."

"Yeah, really, *Days of Thunder?*" said Rob Reiner.

"What the hell is that?" said Larry David. "Is that a movie? I never heard of it."

There was murmuring in the crowd. Evidently no one else had heard of the movie either. In the corner, Nicole Kidman sat quietly staring at the rug. Though it hardly seemed possible, no one realized that this was a movie Nicole herself had starred in, back in 1990, with her then-husband Tom Cruise. It was set in the world of NASCAR and for some reason I remember there was a single associated with it called "Show Me Heaven," performed by the singer Maria McKee, formerly of the cowpunk country rock band Lone Justice.

Finally, the Vermeer spoke.

"It's a race car movie," she said.

Actually she said, "It's a race cah movie," in her Australian accent.

Not everyone heard her, but those who did were still unable to place it.

"A race car movie?" said Larry David. "You mean like *Cannonball Run?*"

"No, more like . . . whatever," said Nicole, waving her hand in dismissal. She pronounced *whatever* as "whateever."

"Well, it's the first I've heard of it," said Larry David.

•

I never saw Nicole Kidman again. My novel was never made
into a movie. I never did a project with the producer Nora
introduced me to at Fred Segal, most likely because I never
bothered to call him. Instead I kept doing essays and journalism and eventually became a columnist at the *Los Angeles
Times*. The screenwriting world was lively and seductive in
ways, but it also felt desperate and slightly sad, as though it
were made up of all the people you knew in high school
who were pretty smart but not the smartest.

"You know what?" said Nora, who'd once been a columnist herself. "You're not a screenwriter, you're a columnist."

It was the highest compliment she could have paid me.

As whatever relationship I'd had with the entertain-
ment business drifted into a passing acquaintanceship, the
map of my particular L.A. took on new contours. I'd lived on
the west side in the beginning, first in Topanga Canyon in the
Santa Monica Mountains, where I might have subconsciously
thought I could replicate some version of that photo of the
Dunne family in Malibu. Later I rented a cottage in funky,
pricey Venice. But I migrated farther east as the years went
on, finally settling among the print journalists and poetry
professors who gravitate toward the less breezy, more afford-
able enclaves near downtown and Pasadena. Here I was among
my own kind. My neighbors weren't just creative types but
also schoolteachers and union organizers and carpenters and
city councilmen. Movie stars did not turn up at the supermarket or anywhere else. People threw backyard barbecues
and stood around and mostly talked about what people anywhere talk about: their kids' schools, their kitchen remodels,
the price of gas.

I bought a house with lemon and orange trees in the yard

and bougainvillea climbing up the fence. At night, police helicopters buzzed overhead, their searchlights slicing through the darkness while coyotes shrieked in the canyons. For the first time in a very long time, I had the sense of being in exactly the right place. For all the ways that I still hadn't shaken New York City out of myself and for all the ways that I missed the broken-down yet good-natured soul of the prairie, I felt oddly, embarrassingly, exhilaratingly Angelino. I planted myself down and felt roots spread out under me like a net. I met people and made friends. I got married. I met even more people and made even more friends, so many that along the way I even picked up a few enemies—or, if not enemies, people who'd rather avoid my company (the feeling is nearly always mutual). I actually see this as an accomplishment, since accruing adversaries is a sure sign that you're a bona fide member of your community. You can't be disliked without being known, and you can't be known without having been around for a while. Los Angeles, if nothing else, is the place I've been hanging around the longest.

In certain moments—driving on the 405 freeway through the brown, flower-flecked hills of the Sepulveda Pass; preparing to dive into the ginlike waters of the pool at the Rosebowl Aquatic Center, where the San Gabriel Valley heat roils off the concrete and my skin gets too tan and my hair bleaches out and some part of me morphs back into the sun-dried child I was in the very beginning—I have to ask myself why it all feels so familiar. Is it a sign that I have truly transformed, that I have become not just *a Californian* but, in a general sense, *Californian*? Or is it simply a resetting of the bones of the Californian I've always been?

I used to have a theory as to why I've suffered fewer

moments of existential uncertainty in California than anywhere else I've lived as an adult and even as a child. It isn't
just that the place is celebrated—again, to the point of cliché
and often unfairly—for its culture of transience and a certain disregard for history. It isn't even that the person I've
been as a Californian has been older, slightly wiser, and
less panicked about paying the rent than the person I was as
a New Yorker and a wannabe Plainswoman. Instead, I'd
decided that the reason the west coast was a place in which
I didn't feel the weight of my inadequacies pressing down
as hard on my sinuses was, quite literally, the weightless-
ness of the air itself.

In most places in the United States, the air is the main
event. In summer in just about every region, it's thick and
soupy and choked with bugs. In winter in the northern states,
the air can be so cold as to shock the system. It's a knife
pressed permanently to your cheek, a constant reminder that
these lands were settled by people who had to eat each other
to stay alive in winter. But in California, particularly in the
waterless, would-be wasteland of the southern half, air is
negligible. The temperature is frequently 78 degrees and remains so whether you're on a street corner waiting for a traffic light to change or in your living room sorting through
the mail. It is possible to go an entire day without realizing
that your back door has been ajar since morning. In that
sense, the line between indoors and outdoors is blurred. The
metaphor then extends to social climates, where being an
insider doesn't have to mean you grew up here or have even
been here very long. It just means you're here right now. It
means you're "present in the moment," as a yoga teacher
would say. It means you can step between insiderness and

outsiderness as easily as walking through a door no one remembers to close.

At least that used to be my theory. Now I just think that
L.A. is a place that's hard to see close up. You can't capture it
from the street. It's an aerial-view kind of city, best photo-
graphed from a helicopter or a hillside. There are people
everywhere, but they are hidden in their cars and houses,
they are tiny specks hiking on the canyon trails, their dogs
even tinier specks beside them, the wildlife crouched in the
sagebrush unnoticed. L.A. is a place that will leave you alone
if you need it to. It will let you cry in your car. It will give
you your space.

A few years after the party at Nora's house, I found myself at a party at Arianna Huffington's house. This time, it
was a huge gathering with easily a hundred guests, few if any
of whom were famous actors as far as I could tell. I'd been
writing my newspaper column for a year or so at that point
and though I'd met Arianna in passing since the charades
party she'd never really registered who I was or what I did.
But now a mutual friend brought me into her circle, where
a flock of reporters and bloggers and other columnists were
cackling away.

"Actually, we played charades together at Nora's," I said
when the friend introduced us.

"Meghan's a columnist at the *L.A. Times*," the friend
said. "I'm sure you've read her."

"Oh, yes!" said Arianna. "You're really good! One of the
best."

It was a savor-the-moment kind of moment. Like when
Nora told me I was not a screenwriter but a columnist. Eventually everything comes together, I thought. Eventually we
all shake out into the thing we were supposed to be all along.

Los Angeles is my home. I am not in the movie business but
I live in L.A. and it is my home.

"Oh my," I said. "Thank you."

"I mean it's not easy," she said, "playing that kind of
charades."

DIARY OF A COMA

October 27, 2010
4:04 p.m.

GENERAL: This is an ill-appearing Caucasian woman.

TYPE OF CONSULTATION: Infectious Disease

PHYSICAL EXAMINATION:
Vital signs: Currently she is afebrile at 36.6 C, pulse 103, respiratory rate 18, and blood pressure 90/60. She is awake and oriented but is a little addled at times and has difficulty finding words.

Acute viral hepatitis is a possibility. Acute hepatitis A is a possibility as is an Epstein-Barr virus (mono-nucleosis syndrome). An enteroviral process such as aseptic meningoencephalitis is another consideration and the patient herself has also raised the possibility of West Nile virus infection. It would be unusual for

Herpes meningoencephalitis to be present with rash, transaminitis, and thrombocytopenia. Primary HIV infection can present in this manner although it seems less likely here. An atypical condition such as murine typhus—especially given her history of prior fleabites—and leptospirosis is to be considered. I doubt this is a bacterial process, but meningococcemia remains on the differential.

First I lost my words. At least that's the first thing I remember when I think about this story, insofar as I *can* think about it, which I try to avoid doing despite the permanent residence it's now taken up in my brain. To experience aphasia is to feel your mind breaking off into pieces, to hear sentences crumbling into useless particles. It is to be so stunned by the fragility of human cognitive function that whatever came before seems almost irrelevant. But of course it's completely relevant.

In the fall of 2010, I was staying at a friend's place in Brooklyn when I got hit with flu symptoms that felt like a truck had driven through the apartment and parked on my head. One minute I felt reasonably okay, if a little sniffly, the next minute I was shivering almost too violently to hold a cup of tea. Still, I assumed it was the flu, as did a doctor friend and the various pharmacists I consulted when I could drag myself out to the drugstore. After three days of trying to keep the fever down with aspirin I flew home to Los Angeles, vomiting once on the plane and becoming so sweaty and overheated that I had to dig through my bag in the overhead compartment to find a T-shirt, a task that depleted so much energy it was another half hour before I could make it to the lavatory to change clothes. The following morning I went to an urgent-care clinic, where I was put on an IV for hydration and told to come back the next day if I wasn't better.

The next day, I could barely walk. My husband took me back to the clinic. In the waiting room, he noticed that the whites of my eyes were yellow. He filled out my registration form because I was too weak to hold a pen. Then he had to leave. He had an interview with a crucial source for a newspaper article he was writing. He'd been trying to set it up for months; there was no rescheduling it.

"Just try to avoid going to the hospital," he said. "People get sick in hospitals."

I was put in an exam room, where I lay on a table getting saline from an IV bag. An hour or more passed. Every so often I pried myself up and took a step across the room, where a Dixie cup sat on the counter. I'd turn on the faucet and fill it with water, knocking it back in one gulp. Then I'd collapse back onto the exam table. This sequence of movements felt equivalent to lifting a car off the ground. But I was thirsty in a way I did not know it was possible to be thirsty. It was as if all the moisture in my body was evaporating. My head was throbbing. My urine was the color of tea. When my mother was dying, "urine the color of tea" was one of the things the hospice workers told me to look out for as a sign of "imminent passing." But I didn't think I was dying. What I was thinking was that the clinic doctor had said I might have hepatitis but that maybe that wasn't the worst thing in the world because, after all, Pamela Anderson has it and she's basically walking around like a normal person.

After a few hours on the saline drip, a nurse came into

the room and told me I was being admitted to the hospital down the street. I said I didn't care where I went as long as I didn't have to get up.

An ambulance took me from the urgent-care clinic to the hospital, a trip of approximately two blocks for which my insurance company would later be billed $860 (and for which it would decline to pay). Though I could already feel myself shrinking back from the world, I tried hard to appear normal, joking around with the paramedics until suddenly I couldn't remember exactly where they said we were going. In the emergency room, I met with an intake nurse who sat by my gurney and took note of every personal item I had with me. Purse, wallet, phone, keys—also my clothes, which had somehow been removed from my body and swapped for a hospital gown, though, like a drunk girl taken home and put to bed by kindly friends after a party, I didn't notice it happening. There was much about the situation that was like being very, very drunk. Far drunker than I'd actually ever been, though I seemed to be following some hardwired personal protocol for saving face, as if I'd been in this predicament before and knew the drill. It took every ounce of concentration to appear coherent. I didn't want to look stupid.

"What is your religious affiliation, if any?" the nurse asked.

"What are my choices?" I tried to say this in a tone that suggested I was being funny, making an ironic little joke. The truth was that I need some prompting.

"Adventist, Baptist, Buddhist, Catholic, Christian, Eastern Orthodox, Episcopalian, Hindu, Jewish, Lutheran, Mormon, Muslim, Presbyterian—"

"Presbyterian," I said. That wasn't true but for some reason I said it anyway. As a teenager, I'd sung in a Presbyterian church choir. My mother had been raised Presbyterian but we did not belong to the church. Later I would see Presbyterian on my chart and think it must be someone else's chart.

And then I got to the part that always seems like the beginning. The part that somehow remains in the present tense even as the whole incident recedes further into the past.

October 27, 2010
4:04 p.m.
"How many fingers am I holding up?" the doctor asks.

I can answer that. That one's easy. Still, there are things that I know and things that I don't. What I know is that I've never felt sicker in my life. Moreover, I've never felt this *kind* of sickness. It's as if my life is draining out of me and pooling at my feet. What I don't know is the degree to which that is indeed an accurate impression. Technically, I am dying. I don't know that a normal platelet count is between 150,000 and 400,000 per microliter and that mine has dropped to 15,000 per microliter. I don't know that my liver and kidneys are seriously compromised and that my BUN, or blood urea nitrogen level, is 35 milligrams per deciliter, far above the normal range of 6 to 20 milligrams per deciliter. I don't know that the doctor is at this moment writing things in my chart such as "scleral icterus," which means that the whites of my eyes are yellow (which I knew earlier but forgot).

Now the doctor is touching my feet and looking at my toes. My toenails are painted a light greenish blue.

"Would you call that cerulean?" he asks.

"I guess you could say that!" I say, too loudly and at too high a pitch. I can't modulate my voice. The harder I try to sound normal, the weirder I sound.

I tell him that I was recently bitten repeatedly in my sleep by a mosquito that was trapped in a New York City apartment I was staying in and still have several welts on my back. I suggest that maybe I have West Nile virus.

The doctor examines my back, peering at the welts like a jeweler peering through a loupe.

"Amazing that you managed to get mosquito bites in New York City in October," he says.

People are always saying this kind of thing to me. I try to explain to the doctor that I'm constantly getting bitten by bugs. It's just something about my body chemistry, not a big deal. I mentioned West Nile more for the purposes of making conversation than out of genuine concern. As a child living in Texas, and even later in New Jersey, I was chronically pocked with mosquito bites that leave scars even now. Once in a motel room in Galveston, a spider bit my eyelid and it was swollen shut for days. These days when I hike in the Sierras, even at high altitudes, I've been known to be singled out by swarms of blackflies so smitten with me that my traveling companions ask if I'm wearing perfume. More recently, a few weeks before the New York trip, I woke up with fleabites all over my ankles, a casualty of letting the dog sleep on the bed. It's not the bites, I tell the doctor. It's hepatitis. I have what Pamela Anderson has.

But I barely have enough energy to pry my lips apart to speak.

The doctor has a rumpled, intellectual air about him, like he could be a graduate student in English. He has a hospital ID and stethoscope around his neck but he is not wearing a lab coat, just a plaid shirt and jeans. He has told me he is an infectious-disease specialist. He is not old but not young. He is maybe in his late forties. I think to myself that he is just the right time for a doctor. What I mean is "just the right age" but "age" does not come to me. Words are floating past me but I cannot grab them. They are slimy fish. They are concepts with letters attached, but the letters are out of order and fading away as if on a screen. I don't want to let on, though. I don't want to embarrass myself in front of the doctor.

Cerulean. I think of color strips from the paint store. I had a cerulean wall once, in a living room somewhere. I painted it myself and it contrasted beautifully with the white wainscoting. This house was a lifetime ago, though it's possible I still live there.

The doctor says he'll order tests and come back later.

RECOMMENDATIONS:
1. Blood cultures will be obtained.
2. CBC, CMT, PT, PTT, chest x-ray, and right upper quadrant ultrasound will be ordered.
3. The patient will be placed on empiric doxycycline and Rocephin.
4. Hepatitis serology, a Mono spot test, and Epstein-Barr virus panel will be ordered.
5. West Nile virus IgM and IgG will be ordered.
6. Weil-Felix antibodies will be obtained.
7. Rickettsial typhi IgM and IgG will be obtained.
8. HIV PCR testing will be ordered.
9. Leptospira antibody will be ordered.

10. As part of comprehensive workup, a lumbar puncture might be helpful, but in this patient the platelet count is currently too low to safely permit this.

October 27, 2010
10:00 p.m.

I am both asleep and not asleep. You know that state where you're not dreaming but, rather, circling semiconsciously around an idea? It's like your mind has been assigned a theme that splits off into a dozen variations as you lie there stuck in hypnagogia. This is the state I am in. The theme I'm working with concerns a friend who is somehow in trouble. I wasn't aware of it before but suddenly I am seized with the knowledge that she is in a very bad way and I have left her to her own devices long enough and now need to tell someone. I've been trying to sleep but the more I lie here, the more I think about her situation and the more it seems like something very bad will happen if I don't get her help now. Also, I am so thirsty that I want to convert my body into a sponge and dunk myself into a vat of water and never come up.

"Hello?" I call. This isn't really the word I mean. "Hello? Hello?"

My husband is here. I think it's maybe the middle of the night, but I'm not sure. I need to tell him about my friend. I had dinner with her when I was in New York last week, right before the fever came on. She is recently married but I am worried for her, though I can't put my finger on why. Like me, she is a freelance writer. I'm not sure if my concern has to do with her career or her personal life. It feels like it's probably both. The word that comes out is *shackles*. Except my words are slurred. It sounds more like "shales" or "shells."

"Sara is in shackles," I say again and again. The slimy fish have turned into oysters in my mouth. They are multiplying. My tongue has shut off its communication receptors and is flopping around in my mouth with the oysters.

My husband says he doesn't know what I'm talking about. I'm making faces and waving my hands around as if we're playing charades.

"What is going on with you?" my husband says. "Do you know where you are right now?"

My husband is talking to someone in the background. Time has gone by. Maybe minutes. Maybe an hour.

"You have to understand, this is not normal," I hear him say. "She uses words for a living. Something is very wrong here."

What I know in real life but have forgotten now is that my husband writes about science and medicine. He almost went to medical school himself. But he went to Africa instead and reported on the Rwandan genocide. Our one-year wedding anniversary was two days ago.

"I think we should call your dad," my husband says.

"Really? What for?" I ask.

October 28, 2010
3:00 a.m.
Dr. Plaid Shirt is back, though he's wearing a different shirt now. I don't know it but it's the middle of the night and my

husband has insisted that the doctor be called at home and ordered to come in.

The doctor covers up his ID and asks, "Who am I?"

"Steve," I say. This is not how he introduced himself earlier but this is what I have to work with. It comes out as "Shteve."

"Fair enough," he says. "What kind of doctor am I?"

I've totally got this. What's more, it's going to impress the hell out of him.

"Epidemiologist," I say. Again with a lisp.

I am under the misimpression that an epidemiologist and an infectious-disease specialist are the same thing. What I mean is that even in my normal, nonconfused state I believe this to be true.

"Okay," the doctor says. He's writing a lot of stuff down. I am worried that he's getting a bad impression of me. He maybe leaves or doesn't leave. Probably he leaves.

Suddenly my toes hurt. Or maybe it's not sudden. Maybe more time has gone by. In any case they hurt a lot. Like they're being frozen off my feet. I still have the nail polish on. I'm kicking my feet and yelling. I'm trying to warm my toes with my hands, except my arm is attached to an IV.

"We have to remove the polish," I hear someone say.

My husband and a nurse are removing the polish. The cerulean is rubbing off onto acetone-soaked cotton balls. The scene fades for me right here, maybe because they give me something to calm me down or maybe because I stop remembering due to natural causes, like falling asleep or passing out. In the ensuing hours, I am transferred to another floor so I can be watched more carefully. I do not know this, though. I am getting closer and closer to not knowing anything at all.

October 28, 2010
Patient transferred to Direct Observation Unit at
5:20 a.m.

9:00 a.m.
TYPE OF CONSULTATION: Neurology

REASON FOR CONSULTATION: Altered Mental Status
40-year-old female patient was admitted yesterday to
the hospital. Her husband as well as a friend are at her
bedside and indicate that yesterday they began to
notice she was having deterioration in her speech. In
fact, she was telling them "I know what I want to say"
but having difficulty getting the words out. She states
that she is in the hospital, however she cannot name
the hospital. She cannot name the president. She is
unable to state the date. She is quite confused.

IMPRESSION:
1. Aphasia with increased deep tendon reflexes in
right lower extremity, suspicious for central nervous
system lesion, rule out ischemic event such as septic
emboli versus encephalitis.

October 28, 2010
2:00 p.m.
I don't know where I am in time or space but I know my husband's close friend is here. She is the woman who married us a
year ago. She got certified on the Internet and officiated at our
ceremony in Central Park, where we stood under a chuppah

even though I am Presbyterian. Now she is saying that the person at the hospital reception desk told her that only family members were allowed in but she that said she was my "clergy person" so they let her in. She is saying she'll go to our house later and feed the dog and bring him to another friend, who will watch him for a few days. She asks if there's anything I need her to do in the house.

I picture the house. It's not really ours but a place we're renting while we look for a real house to buy. It's a little shabby and the yard is overgrown and layered with several seasons of leaves, but we rented it because the landlady allowed dogs. I think about what our friend might do for me in the house and I see a stack of laundry on the dryer. Not a stack but a pile. Some socks probably fell on the floor. I need her to pick the socks up and put them back in the pile. Or maybe in the drawer. The socks need to go from the pile to the drawer, though maybe not back to the pile. Maybe the pile can be skipped.

I try to explain this. The laundry is floating in front of me. Shirt sleeves blowing in the breeze like in a laundry commercial. Underwear folded neatly. Maybe what I want her to do is take stuff out of the dryer. Or actually out of the washer. That's what it is. I want her to take most of the stuff that's in the washer and put in the dryer. Except there are a few things that need to be hung up to dry. One of those things starts with a letter in the alphabet.

"You know the thing I mean," I say. Not only is my speech slurred by now but my voice has melted into a flaccid monotone. I sound like a hobbit in a smial. I sound exactly like my mother sounded when she was dying.

My husband's friend is smiling and nodding as if everything is fine and casual. I don't notice that her face is contorted in fear.

"I understand," she says. "I'll take care of it."

October 28, 2010
6:00 p.m.
Patient moved to ICU after signs of deterioration. Propofol sedation.
Currently, decreased reflexes. Presence of nuchal (neck) rigidity.
Meningioencephalitis, clearly worse than this a.m., discussed at length with husband and brother. Despite DIC/thrombocytopenia I feel potential benefit from lumbar puncture outweighs risks given the clinical deterioration and despite abx and acoclyovir.

Patient to be intubated for airway protection/safety and L/P will hopefully be done later if platelets/coagulants can be improved. Patient's husband understands risks/benefits. Informed consent was obtained for L/P and blood/blood product transfusions. Patient will receive right and left wrist restraints due to agitation/combative behavior.

What I will learn later is that I have been placed in what is essentially a medically induced coma. I will learn that I was thrashing around so much that they had to tie me to the bed with wrist restraints. Then, for sedation and "control of stress responses," they placed me under propofol, the drug Michael Jackson used when he wanted to take naps and that eventually killed him. I am breathing on a ventilator for "airway protection" and I have a feeding tube. The MRI has shown that I have meningoencephalitis, a swelling of the brain and the lining around the brain due to infection. They think the infection is viral, for instance, some kind of massive herpes infection, but the insect bites also raise the possibility that I have West Nile or *Rickettsia typhi*, better known as murine typhus, which is caused by fleas not just biting you but then also defecating on your skin and spreading bacteria through your bloodstream when you scratch.

But the brain infection is not even the main event at this moment. The most pressing issue is that sepsis in my blood-stream has given me something called disseminated intravascular coagulation, or DIC. This means that clots have formed throughout my small vessels and blocked blood flow. The clotting is using up my platelets and creating a risk of massive internal bleeding or external bleeding through the nose or mouth or from under the skin. DIC is a life-threatening condition. Also, my liver and kidneys are now failing.

To complicate things further, I need to undergo a lumbar puncture, or spinal tap, in order to extract central nervous system fluids that will hopefully provide some better clues as to what is wrong with me. But it's dangerous to do a spinal tap on a patient whose platelet count is as low as mine. At first, the doctors decide to delay the lumbar puncture until I receive more platelet transfusions. But when my neck begins to stiffen and my blood-work numbers worsen they confer around midnight and decide they have no choice. My husband is shown a consent form saying he understands that the procedure carries the risk of spontaneous internal bleeding that could lead to permanent paralysis or death. It is explained to him that given how sick I am there's a chance of these outcomes happening anyway. On the other hand, it's also possible that testing the central nervous system fluids will yield no information. My husband, who has never so much as borrowed my credit card and forged my signature, must make the final decision whether or not to proceed. By now, my brother, who lives in town, is at the hospital and my father is on a plane from New York. My husband signs the form. A transport team comes and wheels me away.

Fifteen minutes later they bring me back. My husband and brother ask how it went and are told it didn't go at all. The doctors decided the procedure was too risky after all. Because it's the middle of the night they do not have access to the imaging equipment that could potentially minimize any complications. They will wait until morning. My husband starts to wonder if I'd be better off at a larger hospital, like UCLA or Cedars-Sinai. Despite the hour, he starts calling anyone he can think of who might have a connection to a blood or brain specialist in Los Angeles. He gets someone on the phone who listens to his story and tells him it probably doesn't make a difference at this point. I'm better off staying where I am.

October 29, 2010
8:02 a.m.
Patient intubated and sedated. Febrile overnight, presence of nuchal rigidity.
Highest temp 102.4F. Tachycardiac. On ventilator.

IMPRESSIONS:
Uncertain if she still has pre-renal azotemia due to sepsis.
Most likely intrinsic renal disease, consider small vessel occlusive disease, catastrophic antiphosiphoid syndrome seems possible but unlikely.

Plan:
Perform lumbar puncture with fluoroscopy.
Continue hemodynamic monitoring and neuro checks
every 2 hours.

Medications:
Ampicillin, Vancomycin, Ceftriaxone, Acyclovir.

Notes: This is a complicated and challenging case.
Likely with mosquito bite encephalopathy (West Nile
Virus vs. St. Louis, Eastern Equine, Japanese) compli-
cated by sepsis and DIC.

As a child I often harbored the thought that I wasn't actually
living my life but instead subsisting in a vegetative state. In
this state, the events I experienced as reality were merely
hallucinations that scrolled through my consciousness while
I was strapped to a bed somewhere, saliva dribbling down
my chin as my body matured and then grew old over loose
bands of atrophied muscles. In other words, I imagined myself as I am at this very moment, a swollen, waxy encasement
of failed and failing organ systems, the subject of whispered
conversations among family members in the hallways and
an occasion for frozen lasagnas left for my husband on the
porch steps. I imagined myself as both the author of my life
and a total nonparticipant in it.

In the future, which is to say after I emerge from this
coma and leave this hospital and return to my life, I will still
occasionally indulge this scenario, though what I'll wonder
is whether I actually ever got out of this bed. I'll wonder if
it's possible that I never recovered from the ordeal of late
October 2010 but instead slipped from a medically induced

coma into a real coma and remained there for years. From there, the life I would have lived will reside solely in my mind. All that's happened since then—all the meals and holidays and arguments in the car, all the boxes packed and unpacked, all the people and pets buried and cremated, all the revolutions of the warming earth around the unblinking sun—will be nothing more than vivid, interminable dreams. Meanwhile, my family will endure a living hell in which there is no legal avenue for removing my feeding tube or otherwise hastening my death.

Weeks from now, my husband will tell me that the outcome he feared most was that I would wake up and be severely impaired. He feared that I wouldn't be the same person. He will tell me that when the doctors told him there was a chance I'd need years of cognitive rehabilitation and, even then, there were no guarantees, he thought that as much as he didn't want me to die that if the worst-case scenario came true it was perhaps better if I did. I will find this all very disturbing but also be in complete agreement. The worst-case scenario would not have been dying. It would have been remaining partially alive.

This period of grim prognosis lasts approximately forty-eight hours. During this time, a friend is charged with the task of getting regular updates from my husband and e-mailing those updates to all of my other friends. The names of these friends have been culled largely from the address book on my cell phone, which contains not just close associates but also people I haven't spoken with in years or, in some cases, people I barely know but whose contact information happens to be in my phone. The result is that everyone from my best friend to my college roommate to a Pilates trainer I worked with exactly once is receiving e-mails about my platelet count. Some are replying. Some are sending flowers

and food and calling my husband incessantly. Some are showing up at the hospital even though they can't enter the inten-
sive care unit and forcing my husband to come out and deal
with them. Some are preparing themselves for news that I
have died. Some are thinking it can't possibly be as serious as
these updates are suggesting.

Some are praying, even some you wouldn't expect it from.
A dear friend who's a conservative evangelical Christian has
got her husband and her kids and her Bible study group and
most of her church begging Jesus to heal me. But there are
others, too. Secularists in Brooklyn apartments and Florida
condos and midcentury-modern houses in hip Los Angeles
neighborhoods are holding their heads in their hands and
murmuring. They say they're praying for me but chances are
they're really praying for themselves. They're praying that
whatever is happening to me never happens to them or anyone they share a bed with or tuck into bed at night. Which
is exactly what I'd be praying for in their situation.

Some are concocting strange fantasies about caring for
me. One will admit later that she imagined feeding me with
a spoon and rubbing my back while teaching me how to say
"cat" and "dog." My best friend, who for years has joked about
someday writing a memoir called "Dead Meghan" so as to
join the esteemed ranks of female writers spilling the secrets
of writer best friends who die prematurely, tries to cheer up
my husband by saying she hasn't started the book yet.

"I'm optimistic for her recovery," she says. "Otherwise
I'd be on page ten by now."

My husband thinks this is funny. Apparently, he actually
laughs. I have married the right man. I have married a man
who has followed every step of my clinical course and engaged with medical personnel on a sometimes excruciat-

ingly detailed level and yet still laughed at this joke. Also, I have a best friend who is capable of uncommon humor and deep humanity. In the past I have forgotten this from time to time but when I wake up I will know it more than I've ever known it. When I wake up I will tell myself I'll never forget it again, though of course I will.

October 30, 2010
6:00 a.m.
Patient still intubated/sedated.
CFS consistent with a viral process or partially bacterial process (probably less likely).
Neck supple again, the nuchal rigidity of last p.m. is much better, scattered purpura on dorsal of hands, feet warmer and better perfused.

A few months from now I will visit my evangelist Christian friend and her husband will pull me aside and tell me how great it is to see me and how worried they were when I was sick.

"You had a lot of people praying for you," he'll say.

"I know," I'll say. "And I really appreciate it."

"I mean, a *lot* of people," he'll say.

"Yes. It was great. Really nice."

"I'm just wondering," he'll say, "if it's changed the way you think about things. If you've given any more thought to faith and the power of prayer."

I will be caught so off guard that I'll say something not only insufficient but ridiculously out of character. I will say that a lot of people were praying who didn't necessarily do so regularly and that there must have been a lot of "healing energy" going on. I will feel like a total ingrate. To these friends, my failure to become a follower of Jesus—to even show a sliver of interest in Jesus—in the wake of my miraculous survival must be the ultimate slap in the face. It's as if I commissioned them for a job and then refused to pay even when they delivered excellent service ahead of schedule.

Other people will ask me what it's like to nearly die. Is there a light? Did I feel the presence of divine or otherworldy love? Did I make a conscious decision to "fight back and live?" I won't know what to say to that, either. The only thing I'll be able to say is that it was like nothing. In this particular situation at least, dying would have been like falling off a log. Actually, it wouldn't even have been that dramatic. It would have been like flipping a light switch when your eyes are already closed. It would have merely been a matter of going from unconsciousness to nonexistence. For years afterward, that will be the thing that scares me most: that I could have just as easily slipped that way as this. "If anyone asks, tell them dying is hard," my mother said to me in her last weeks. For me, at least in late October 2010, dying would have been a piece of cake.

October 31, 2010
9:02 a.m.
Attempted to wake patient up, sedation at minimum, patient moves around but does not follow commands.

11:00 a.m.
Off propofol since 9 a.m. Patient moving extremities but not responding to verbal stimulation.

Later I will find out the neurologist is yelling, "Wake up!" directly in front of my face and I am not responding. This is of particular concern because meningoencephalitis can cause deafness. My husband will tell me that they're getting out my iPod and putting the buds in my ears and blasting Joni Mitchell (as if Joni is the kind of artist you can "blast") and still not getting a reaction. I will find this both highly disturbing and strangely mortifying.

November 1, 2010
4:30 a.m.
Patient agitated, eyes open, not fully conscious.
Patient appears to have made positive progress, fever reducing.

9:01 a.m.
Awake, follows commands.

11:20 a.m.
Follows commands, sort of oriented, knows name.
When asked what year it is states "2011."
Knows she's in hospital but cannot name which one.
When prompted "Huntington" she says "gardens/beach."

It's morning. Last night they took my toenail polish off and now I'm waking up. At least that's the situation as far as I'm concerned. They're telling me that four days have passed, but this doesn't compute even slightly. The last four days don't exist for me, though they will haunt my husband for the rest of his life. I see my father standing over my bed and think he must have just arrived on an early flight.

Someone is asking me what year it is and I am saying it's 2011 and not 2010. The hospital is called Huntington but there is also a Huntington Botanical Gardens and, more relevant to me, a Huntington Beach, where dogs can run off-leash and where I've taken my dog and watched him roll in the sand in pure canine ecstasy. So when they say "Huntington" I say "Beach." In a few days my husband will bring in a photo of the dog and put it near my bed where I can see it at all times.

Five days from now, when I'm still in the hospital but no longer in the ICU, the test from the central nervous system fluid will come back positive for murine typhus. This will mean that my infection is bacterial rather than viral. It will mean that it wasn't the mosquito that made me sick (or herpes or Japanese spotted fever or leptospirosis or HIV or any of the other candidates) but, rather, the flea feces that I embedded in myself when I scratched my feet. The fleas are living on rats and opposums in the overgrown yard of the rental house and they got on the dog and then on me. This will be reported to the county health department and someday I'll even record a "survivor's testimony" video for a flea-borne-typhus symposium at the Mosquito and Vector Control Association of California's annual meeting. In the meantime, the doctors will remain mystified by how I managed to get so sick from something that usually just gives people flu symptoms for a few days and then goes away. Moreover, they will be shocked at how quickly I got better. It will be as if grave illness were a deep swimming hole I plunged down to the bottom of and then shot back out of at the last possible second. They will tell me I scared them. A patient care coordinator who read my chart when I was in the ICU will come into my room and tell me that it's quite literally a miracle that I've recovered. The neurologist will also use the word *miracle*. This will give me chills. Neurologists shouldn't use words like *miracle*. Only evangelical Christians should. And even then they should choose their audiences wisely.

November 1, 2010
9:30 a.m.
Clinically dramatically better, DIC is resolving.
Remove D/C foley catheter, transfer out of ICU to medical surgical floor.

My husband is holding my hand. His face is down in my face.
"You were so sick," he says. "But you're going to be okay."
I am relieved by this, though I have no idea just how relieved I should be. I try to speak but it's like my facial muscles are buried under wet cement. I open my eyes and close them. Time passes. I tell myself that if I'm lucky enough to wake all the way up I will become a better person. Even in this state of unprecedented grogginess, even though I am not really awake yet but gliding toward consciousness on a slowly melting, invisible ice floe, I have the idea that this is the kind of thing I'm supposed to be saying to myself. I feel some mandate to take an inventory of all the meaningless crap I was caught up in before I got sick—the real estate market, the vagaries of my career, the merciless judgments I'm capable of casting upon everyone and everything in my wake—and realize how silly and shortsighted I was.

Except even on the ice floe, I know this is a fantasy. As I inch toward the shore, I am collecting the pieces of myself that were swept away with the tide but are floating back to me now. I am reclaiming my words. I am locating the letters of the alphabet and arranging them so that they correspond with the ideas in my head. I am coming back to myself. And

I am no wiser or more evolved than I was before. There is no epiphany or revelation or aha moment or big click. There is no redemption. There is no great lesson learned. There is only the unknowable and the unspeakable. There is only the un-likely if ever-present possibility that life is just a string of sto-ries inside a coma. And in this story, I am not a better person. I am the same person. This is a story with a happy ending. Or at least something close enough.

ACKNOWLEDGMENTS

I am awed by and indebted to Alex Star, who edited this book with a level of rigor and acumen that is increasingly rare in publishing. He is an old-school editor, a true intellectual whose patience, kindness, and good humor make his writers forget how much smarter he is than they are (or at least than this one is). Thanks also to Laird Gallagher, Delia Casa, Elisa Rivlin, Sarah Scire, and Matt Wolfson for sweating the many, *many* details and to Kimberly Burns for being so amazing at what she does.

This book began with "Matricide," and I have Lisa Glatt and David Hernandez to thank for talking me out of my original plan of keeping it in a drawer for the rest of my life. They also made helpful editorial suggestions about that essay and encouraged me to come up with more like it. Heather Havrilesky was another early reader and had many wise things to say, as she does in many areas of life.

Tina Bennett has been my ally and advocate for more than ten years and I feel lucky every day knowing that she and the irreplaceable Svetlana Katz are on my side.

My editors at the *Los Angeles Times*, Susan Brenneman,

Sue Horton, and Nick Goldberg, were kind enough to give me time off and not hire a permanent replacement while I finished this project. I appreciate that space immensely as well as the space they've made for my opinions all these years.

I was privileged to write parts of this book at the Mac-Dowell Colony and at Yaddo, both of which granted me the luxury of time, meals, and rooms of my own.

Thanks, finally, to Alan Zarembo, whose patience, love, and partnership are an extraordinary gift.

A NOTE ABOUT THE AUTHOR

Meghan Daum is a columnist for the *Los Angeles Times* and the author of three previous books, including the essay collection *My Misspent Youth*. Her essays and reviews have appeared in *The New Yorker*, *Harper's Magazine*, *Vogue*, and other publications, and she has contributed to NPR's *Morning Edition*, *Marketplace*, and *This American Life*. Visit her website at MeghanDaum.com.